YOUNGSTOWN'S
DEPENDABLE STORE

Strouss'

Thomas Welsh & Michael Geltz

With the Mahoning Valley Historical Society

Charleston • London

THE
History
PRESS

Published by The History Press
Charleston, SC 29403
www.historypress.net

Copyright © 2012 by Thomas G. Welsh Jr. and Michael K. Geltz
All rights reserved

First published 2012

Manufactured in the United States

ISBN 978.1.60949.799.6

Library of Congress CIP data applied for.

Dedicated to fond memories of Susan E. Welsh and Doris D. "Dolly" Geltz.

"People live in cities, not states or nations."

—*Eduardo Paes, mayor of Rio de Janeiro*

Contents

Acknowledgements

This project benefited from the guidance and support of numerous colleagues, friends and relatives. We would like to offer special thanks to H. William Lawson, executive director of the Mahoning Valley Historical Society, for permitting the use of scores of historical images from the organization's collection. We would also like to thank Pamela Speis, archivist for the Mahoning Valley Historical Society, who provided invaluable assistance at the early stages of this project. Mrs. Speis not only tracked down volumes of material related to the history of the Strouss-Hirshberg Co. but also assisted in the selection of images that would eventually be included in this volume.

Also worthy of appreciation are the many people who agreed to be interviewed regarding their memories of Strouss' Department Store and Youngstown's former retail district. Interviewees included Janet DeCapua, James Gray Doran, Anthony Dudzik, C. Clark Hammit, Reverend Deacon John C. Harris, Josephine Houser, Sally Joseph, Ray Laret, Ben Lariccia, Concetta Lariccia, Amelia Marinelli, Terry O'Halloran, Richard S. Scarsella, Mary Ann Senediak, Patricia Sveth and Betty Swanson. Notably, Reverend Harris extended the additional courtesy of permitting us to use photographs he took in the vicinity of Strouss' Department Store in the 1980s. Likewise, Ben Lariccia and his aunt, Concetta Lariccia, shared family photographs related to the store's history. In addition, Mary Lou Moss Godleski was kind enough to share with us a reproduction of a commemorative booklet that had been presented to her great-aunt, Ann Moss, by the Strouss-Hirshberg

Co. at the time of the firm's golden jubilee in 1925. While conducting general research for this project, we benefited from the assistance of the following individuals: Debbie Bushmire, Sally Freaney, Michele Mellor and Hannah Moses, reference librarians at Youngstown's Reuben-McMillan Public Library. We owe a special word of appreciation to Elaine M. Welsh, who, among others, served as an excellent (and remarkably patient) proofreader.

Thomas G. Welsh and Michael K. Geltz
October 18, 2012
Youngstown, Ohio

INTRODUCTION

"Built for the Future"

O n the afternoon of November 2, 1926, a lone biplane hovered over the $2.5 million complex of the Strouss-Hirshberg Co. in downtown Youngstown, Ohio. As an excited crowd gathered below, the airplane swooped toward West Federal Street, the heart of the city's retail district, while the pilot released a cardboard box attached to a silk parachute. "It had been planned to have it sail gracefully into the street," the *Youngstown Vindicator* reported later that day, "but the winds out of the canyon-like street caused the parachute to travel north." The box instead nestled, rather unceremoniously, on a cornice of the new building, and as a department store worker scrambled to retrieve it, Youngstown mayor Charles F. Scheible waited patiently at the building's main entrance, surrounded by a clutch of city officials.

When the box finally reached him, the mayor promptly opened it, removed a floral wreath and presented it to Clarence J. Strouss Sr., president and general manager of the Strouss-Hirshberg Co., now one of the largest retail outlets in the city.[1] Despite the obvious glitch in the mayor's plans, this piece of showmanship was consistent with the spirit of the occasion. The residents of Youngstown, after all, had anticipated the completion of this state-of-the-art department store for eight years. In November 1918, the Strouss-Hirshberg Co. announced it had secured a ninety-nine-year lease for what many retailers saw as the city's most valuable real estate, and the building project that ensued involved the demolition of several downtown landmarks.[2]

Therefore, few were surprised when hundreds of people showed up for the department store's grand opening, and the moment Clarence Strouss accepted the mayor's floral tribute, the crowd surged forward, forcing members of the city's traffic squad to raise their batons and push back. After a brief struggle, the store was officially opened to the public, and the crowd streamed into the building's main floor.[3] These first-time visitors were undoubtedly dazzled by the sights that awaited them.

Designed by the prestigious architectural firm of Starrett & Van Vleck, the Strouss-Hirshberg Co. building offered a taste of East Coast sophistication to a city that was still struggling against its reputation as a scrappy industrial town. The building's neo-Renaissance façade, which stretched more than 118 feet along West Federal Street, featured cream-colored, semi-glazed terra cotta. Even in the pale light of autumn, the department store was a gleaming presence in the city's downtown. Twenty-two display windows graced the structure's northern and southern entrances, and those who entered the ground floor found twenty-two-foot ceilings and flooring composed of Italian travertine, a form of limestone that the *Vindicator* termed "as durable as marble without the danger of slipping."

The six-story building, which was designed for the addition of two more stories, offered a total floor space of 239,803 square feet, while the basement alone contained 25,000 square feet. The facility was illuminated by 1,553 lamps, and its sprawling electrical system powered five passenger elevators, two freight elevators and spiral-chute conveyors that were intended to speed the delivery of packages. In addition, the building was outfitted with an intricate network of pneumatic tubes, "enabling salespeople to dispatch money to central cashiers as well as charge checks direct with express train speed." The fifth floor featured a massive fur vault in which $1 million worth of furs could be stored, while the sixth floor contained an auditorium capable of seating five hundred people.

Standing guard on the structure's roof were two massive tanks holding twenty-five thousand gallons of water each and a smaller one that held ten thousand gallons. "Wells sunk 150 feet under the foundation of the building, supply water to electric pumpers which lift it to water softeners and then into huge reservoirs upon top of the building," the *Vindicator* reported, one day prior to the grand opening. "They serve the sprinkler system protecting

Previous page: This illustration, which appeared in one of Strouss-Hirshberg's in-house publications, reflects the pride the company took in its flagship store. *Courtesy of Mahoning Valley Historical Society*.

the structure in the event of fire," the paper observed, exclaiming that the store had been "built for the future"—a future that would, in all probability, involve the city's continued expansion. "The new store is not built for the Youngstown of 160,000 souls today, but for the great industrial center of tomorrow with a population of 300,000," the *Vindicator* stated.[4]

More than eight decades later, the former Strouss-Hirshberg building still dominates Youngstown's West Federal Street, although the department store and its branches have long disappeared from the scene. Indeed, the city's once vibrant downtown is still recovering from the combined effects of suburbanization, depopulation and deindustrialization, which reduced the district to a veritable wasteland in the late 1980s and the 1990s. It's apparent that the heady predictions of the 1920s never were realized, and Youngstown's population, at 66,982, stands at less than half of what it was when the Strouss-Hirshberg complex first opened its doors. Yet, memories of the Strouss-Hirshberg Department Store (or Strouss', as it became known in later years) remain vivid in the minds of area residents and former residents alike.

In a recent interview, local educator and public historian Richard Scarsella reflected on the glory days of the 1950s and early 1960s, when the downtown was the bustling hub of the community. "In downtown…there was a mixture of colors and sounds, and there was quite a bit of foot traffic," he recalled. "You'd see street people with their shopping bags. You could see young mothers with their children in carriages. You'd see teenagers killing time, and you would see the professional people that worked downtown in the banks, the office towers, rushing around, usually on their lunch hour or their coffee break, trying to get something to eat very quickly." For observers like Scarsella, the district resembled nothing so much as "a slice of New York City."[5]

Even some of those who have relocated, like Philadelphia resident Ben Lariccia, affectionately recall the excitement involved in a bus trip to downtown Youngstown. Lariccia still remembers peering out the windows of the East High Avenue trolley bus, as the modest homes of his gritty east-side neighborhood receded in the distance, only to be replaced by sparkling retail outlets whose displays highlighted fashions from New York and Chicago. "I guess you might say the trip from Bennington Avenue on the east side was more like going from the country into the city," he said.[6]

For many of those who visited downtown Youngstown in the late 1940s and 1950s, Strouss' Department Store was a primary destination, and the trip was always an occasion. "Women wore hats and gloves and were nicely dressed," recalled Josephine Houser, a retired marriage and family counselor. "And you walked into this lovely store and everything was neat and clean, and everything was orderly. It was not jammed with…racks, like we see today—and…customer service was unbelievable."[7] Mary Ann Senediak, who knew the store as both a customer and an employee, savors the memory of Strouss' signature chocolate malts, whose unique flavor and texture have never been duplicated by local concessionaires, despite widely publicized claims.[8]

Sentimental reveries like these are common in "Rust Belt" communities like Youngstown, which were devastated by the retreat of staple industries in the 1970s and 1980s. In recent years, however, concentrated efforts to preserve the memory of local icons like Strouss' Department Store have unfolded in the context of the steady revitalization of Youngstown's once-desolate core. Since the early twenty-first century, the downtown has benefited from the establishment of small businesses, including restaurants, delicatessens, galleries and consignment shops.

This positive trend became most evident after 2004, which saw the removal of the Federal Plaza, a well-intentioned 1970s effort to revitalize the district by making it more pedestrian-friendly. In Youngstown, as elsewhere, the blocking-off of major thoroughfares had actually hastened the decline of downtown-area businesses, and hence, the reopening of these streets proved to be the first in a series of events that inspired talk of a "downtown renaissance."[9] One year later, in 2005, a high-tech convocation center called the Chevrolet Centre (now known as the Covelli Centre) opened on the site of an abandoned steel mill located southeast of Youngstown's main square.[10] These events coincided with more subtle developments in the community's technology sector. Five years earlier, in 2000, the Youngstown Business Incubator (YBI) began supporting business-to-business software companies, and before long, the incubator had developed and restored a once-decaying block of West Federal Street.

In July 2009, *Entrepreneur* magazine included Youngstown in a list of the top ten U.S. cities in which to open a new business.[11] That same year, the city announced that a private developer, armed with federal and state funding, would restore the Realty Building, a historic skyscraper on Youngstown's Federal Square, transforming it into an upscale apartment building.[12] Then, in December 2011, it was announced that a $9 million project would turn the downtown's long-vacant Erie Terminal Building into a sixty-five-person residential complex.[13]

These changes have brought new hope to many of those who remember the color and vitality of Youngstown's traditional core. While retail outlets remain a "missing piece" of the district's ongoing revitalization, suburbanites who once avoided the downtown now speak enthusiastically about its imminent comeback. "I couldn't wait to go downtown when I started hearing about these restaurants and so forth," said Amelia Marinelli, who worked in the downtown area during the 1940s and 1950s. "I tell you, I'm not even part of it, and I'm excited for them…because I remember the downtown."[14]

Even local civic leaders, who once lamented the "backward-looking" nature of local discourse, are actively encouraging explorations of the community's past, which they have come to see as a partial blueprint for future development. Patricia Sveth, who worked at Strouss' Department Store as a young floater (part-time worker) in the 1970s, touched on this phenomenon when she described the importance of remembering the "old" downtown. "That whole downtown experience was so much a part of the first, at least, fifteen years of my life," she said. "And I really think that it gives us a sense of…what is possible, and that there was a time when people, I think, were more civil to each other and were more concerned about human contact."[15]

These sentiments are shared by former resident Ben Lariccia, who suggested that "cities, like languages, are some of the greatest accomplishments of the human race." For observers like Lariccia, urban centers are least attractive when "there's no place where people cross and meet and develop a connection."[16]

Traditional downtowns provided just such a meeting place, and there seems to be a growing consensus that the vacuum left in the wake of their steep decline has yet to be filled, despite the rapid growth of suburban communities. Positive trends that have swept downtown Youngstown provide an important context for this historical narrative, which draws on sources including internal memos, newsletters, annual reports, personal letters, newspaper articles and oral history interviews with individuals who worked and shopped at the store. While much effort has been made to produce a detailed and engaging account of the flagship store in Youngstown, a certain amount of space has also been devoted to the division's various branches in Ohio and Pennsylvania.

Chapter one, "Origins of a Local Icon," focuses on the department store's founders, Isaac Strouss and Bernard Hirshberg, as well as their influential mentor, David Theobald, a pioneer in Youngstown's retail sector. As the chapter shows, Theobald was largely responsible for Strouss's presence in Youngstown, given that he agreed to meet the young immigrant (a distant relative) in New York City and promptly took him on as an employee. It was Theobald who first exposed Strouss to cutting-edge business practices at a time when many residents of the Mahoning

Valley still engaged in traditional bartering. The retailer even facilitated Strouss's fateful meeting with Hirshberg, as both men were employed at Theobald's firm. The first chapter follows the business partners' continual successes, from their purchase of Theobald's Little Woolen Store in 1875 to their lavish celebration of the store's golden anniversary in 1925—an event that dovetailed with the construction of the Strouss-Hirshberg Co.'s new edifice on West Federal Street.

The grand opening of the new facility, in 1926, is described in chapter two, "A Metropolitan Enterprise," which highlights the career of Isaac Strouss's son, Clarence Strouss Sr., a tireless worker who established three branch stores before the close of the 1920s. As Clarence Strouss led the department store through the challenging years of the Great Depression, he built on his late father's business model, which emphasized outstanding customer service and respectful employee relations. Prior to his untimely death, he laid the groundwork for the store's dramatic post–World War II expansion.

Chapter three, "Postwar Boom," describes the thriving downtown retail outlet that many Youngstown natives still recall with affection. In the wake of a 1948 merger with the Cleveland-based May Company, the Strouss' Division (as it became known) retained a robust local identity and continued to operate under local management. At the same time, the division established multiple branches, whose successes enabled it to upgrade store facilities, broaden selections and meet the needs of the growing number of customers residing in suburban neighborhoods. Despite the expansion of outlying communities and a leveling off of Youngstown's population, Strouss' Department Store remained the centerpiece of a vibrant downtown retail district throughout the 1950s. Indeed, the negative effects of suburbanization and depopulation would not become apparent until at least a decade later.

These trends are examined in chapter four, "Soaring into the Sixties and Seventies," which describes the gradual decline of Youngstown's downtown area, a development that dovetailed with the rise of shopping malls and suburban plazas. In the late 1970s and early '80s, this downward trend would be dramatically accelerated by the collapse of the region's steel industry. Such developments are explored in chapter five, "Rainbow's End," which focuses on the Strouss' Division's final years, a period that culminated with a nullifying merger and the symbolic closure of the flagship store in downtown Youngstown.

Throughout, this narrative includes the voices of those who remember the experience of shopping in a traditional department store, one that offered amenities that are rarely found in modern-day retail outlets. Hopefully this

The third edifice of Strouss-Hirshberg Co. was sold off when the firm opened its new $2.5 million state-of-the-art department store in 1926. *Courtesy of Mahoning Valley Historical Society.*

detailed reconstruction of the history of Strouss' Department Store will offer readers more than "a stroll down memory lane." With luck, it will also serve as part of a usable past, whose lessons can be employed in the present—and the future.

CHAPTER 1

Origins of a Local Icon

Under the solemn gaze of an honor guard, hundreds of people streamed into the main auditorium of Youngstown's Temple Rodef Sholom, each attendant pausing respectfully at the funeral bier of Isaac Strouss. The seventy-seven-year-old retailer had suffered a stroke within days of the fiftieth anniversary of the Strouss-Hirshberg Co., and several weeks later, on the morning of April 1, 1925, he quietly passed away at the north-side home (located a few blocks from the temple) of his daughter, Mrs. I. Harry Meyer.

In early March, Strouss and his longtime business partner, Bernard Hirshberg, had participated in a gala celebration of their enterprise's golden anniversary, which drew six hundred guests to the city's well-appointed YMCA building. Given the circumstances, Strouss's final illness was treated in the media as a product of the "nervous tension and excitement of the occasion."[17]

Whatever the case, many of those who had gathered for the store's jubilee celebration found themselves meeting once again—this time to pay tribute to the memory of the Strouss-Hirshberg Co.'s driving force. Among them was Strouss's friend and business rival, Lucius B. McKelvey (president of McKelvey's Department Store), who would serve as an honorary pallbearer at the funeral service.[18] Meanwhile, the eulogy would be given by Dr. I.E. Philo, rabbi of Rodef Sholom, who had delivered the keynote address at the Strouss-Hirshberg jubilee banquet.[19]

In the two days that had elapsed since Strouss's death, dozens of tributes were reprinted in the local newspapers, and while many were composed in the stiff, florid prose of the era, their sheer number suggested the esteem

Isaac Strouss as he appeared around the time that Strouss-Hirshberg Co. marked its golden jubilee. *Courtesy of Mahoning Valley Historical Society.*

in which Strouss was held by leading citizens of his adopted hometown. Beyond the pro forma references to the subject's "benevolence," "broad-mindedness," "tolerance" and "public-mindedness," many tributes focused on Strouss's "gentleness" and "humility," qualities one might not immediately connect with a successful entrepreneur.

What emerges from a review of the tributes is a rough sketch of a man who never lost sight of his humble roots, who remembered those who had helped him and who was not inclined to take his success for granted. "In his store, he was as inconspicuous as an office boy," wrote local columnist Esther Hamilton, in an article printed in the *Youngstown Telegram* on the day of the funeral. "His authority was felt, not seen," she added.[20]

Ms. Hamilton illustrated the point with an anecdote involving an impatient customer who "flounced" into the Strouss-Hirshberg Co. and demanded to be directed to the table-linen department. According to the story, a gentleman who was standing nearby approached the woman and led her to the department in question, "where he personally waited on her, dragging down bolt after bolt and box after box to satisfy the woman's whims." In the end, the man met her requirements, making a sale of more than $100. "He made out the bill as patient and smiling as tho [*sic*] the woman had been a lady instead of a person out only to get her money's worth at the expense of trampling down the common people," Ms. Hamilton wrote. The gentleman who waited on the demanding customer was, of course, Isaac Strouss—by that time one of Youngstown's most prominent merchants.

Whether or not the anecdote was true, it conveyed an image of Strouss that resonated with many who knew him, including longtime employees. According to the *Telegram*, those who worked at the Strouss-Hirshberg Co. indicated that "in all their years of service with him, he was never known to utter an unkind or harsh word." Mistakes, along with evidence of indifference, "brought forth advice from him that was couched in words of wisdom and kindliness."[21]

By the time of his death, most Youngstown-area residents were familiar with the broad outlines of Isaac Strouss's life story. They had heard about his youthful decision to leave a tiny German village for an unknown country, his eventful sea voyage, his fateful meeting with a cousin who lived in Ohio and his astonishingly successful partnership with fellow immigrant Bernard Hirshberg. This story had been recounted, with obvious pride, by his son, Clarence J. Strouss (a popular public speaker and sportsman), who assumed the presidency of the Strouss-Hirshberg Co. in 1924, one year before his father's death. "When a German lad seventeen years of age said 'Goodbye' to mother, father and other loved ones…little did they think of the part that he was destined to play in the commercial life of a small American town in Ohio," Clarence Strouss had written in 1913. "After tossing about the ocean for some six or seven weeks in an old-fashioned sailing vessel, swept out of her course by a storm, this boy finally landed in New York. Little if any money was there in his pockets as he was met on the dock by a distant relative."[22] In its barest form, this narrative features the basic elements of a Horatio Alger story, one in which the protagonist achieves success by dint of willpower and perseverance. While this interpretation is not entirely unjustified, Isaac Strouss was inclined to tell his own story a little differently, with a greater emphasis on the people who had assisted him over the years.

Strouss's obituary indicates that he was born to Jacob and Helena Mayer Strouss in the village of Hahnheim, on May 20, 1848. Hahnheim, at that time, was located in the state of Rheinhessen, which encompassed Germany's largest wine region. (Post–World War II boundary changes now place the village within the federal state of Rheinland-Pfalz.) Relatively little has been passed down about Strouss's formative years in Germany, beyond the fact that he attended local public schools and "became a proficient student of the French language."[23]

At some point, the teenaged Strouss became involved in a correspondence with David Theobald, a cousin who hailed from Helena Strouss's hometown of Ilbesheim, Bavaria. Theobald, more than twenty years older than Isaac Strouss, had left Germany back in 1849. After working for a couple of years as a retail clerk in New Castle, Pennsylvania, Theobald moved on to neighboring Youngstown, Ohio, where he established his own clothing store in 1852. Eight years later, in 1860, he formed a business partnership with another German-born entrepreneur, Ferdinand Ritter, and the pair went on to organize David Theobald & Co., one of Youngstown's largest commercial firms.[24] Decades later, and some years after Theobald's death, a local newspaper stated, "To write of the business firms and business men of Youngstown without mention of D. Theobald & Co....would be like writing of Italy and failing to mention the Alps."[25] Overall, it would be difficult to imagine a more fortuitous contact for an aspiring young merchant like Isaac Strouss.

In 1865, when Theobald learned of Strouss's imminent arrival at Castle Garden, he scheduled a buying trip in New York City, which enabled him to meet his young relative at the dock. Irving E. Ozer and his coauthors described the scene as follows: "Taken in charge by Theobald, the young immigrant was first escorted to a barber shop and given an American haircut, and then, after being fitted in a 'salt and pepper' business suit, he was ready to learn something about 'business.'"[26] Strouss watched closely as his cousin (a large man with a commanding presence) toured New York City's Garment District and purchased his entire stock of fall goods. When business was concluded, the pair boarded a train for Youngstown, and Theobald offered Strouss a position

ONE PRICE HOUSE. ESTABLISHED IN 1852.

D. THEOBALD & CO.,

Merchant Tailors,

WHOLESALE AND RETAIL

CLOTHIERS.

AGENTS FOR ALL

Leading Sewing Machines and Attachments.

AGENTS FOR THE

QUAKER CITY AND KING OF ALL SHIRTS.

23 West Federal Street,

YOUNGSTOWN, OHIO.

Pioneer retailer David Theobald placed this advertisement in the Youngstown City Directory in 1877. *Courtesy of Mahoning Valley Historical Society.*

at a starting wage of four dollars a week. Since the teenager spoke little, if any, English, his first duties were limited to "sweeping out the premises, tending to the oil lamps, putting coal on the fire and unpacking boxes."

The ambitious youth, however, soon became familiar with the store's stock, and before long "he was seizing every opportunity to sell collars, ties and such other articles of apparel as he could pronounce and which were not too difficult to sell."[27] As his English language skills improved, Strouss began to sell items door-to-door in Youngstown and its outskirts, an experience that helped him internalize some of the basic rules of business.[28]

It would be difficult to overstate the degree to which David Theobald influenced the life of young Isaac Strouss. Well regarded within Youngstown's growing business sector, Theobald was also a leader within the city's small, close-knit Jewish community, which then consisted mostly of German and Austrian immigrants. In 1867, two years after Strouss's arrival, Theobald

The first edifice of Temple Rodef Sholom stood a few blocks north of Youngstown's downtown. Isaac Strouss and Bernard Hirshberg were founding members of the congregation. *Courtesy of Mahoning Valley Historical Society.*

was among fifteen men who met at the home of fellow retailer Abraham Walbrun to approve the bylaws and constitution of the city's first Jewish congregation, Rodef Sholom ("Pursuer of Peace").[29] One year later, in 1868, Theobald opened a subscription list and established a sinking fund for the purchase of property on which a Reform temple would be built. Then, in 1886, he presided over the dedication of the temple's first edifice, located a few blocks north of downtown Youngstown.[30]

Not surprisingly, many of the prominent families within the local Jewish community were connected by marriage, a pattern no less evident within Youngstown's white Protestant elite. In Theobald's case, his partnership with Ferdinand Ritter was no doubt strengthened by his marriage to Ritter's sister, Caroline. Ritter, meanwhile, was married to Theobald's sister, Minie.[31] Later on, Theobald would introduce young Strouss to his own daughter's attractive sister-in-law, Lena Pfaelzer, a resident of Philadelphia.

By the early 1870s, Strouss had developed into a striking young man with thick hair and a stylish mustache. His social confidence was undoubtedly bolstered by his success as a salesman, which helped him to secure a position at A. Walburn & Co., a firm in which Theobald owned an interest. In 1872, Theobald became sole owner of the business, and two years later, in 1874, Strouss was elevated to the position of store manager.[32] At that point, the firm became known as the Woolen Store, although it would later be referred to as the Little Woolen Store, as if to highlight Strouss's humble beginnings as a retailer. By then, Strouss had already befriended another young worker named Bernard Hirshberg, who was employed as a bookkeeper for Theobald's firm. Like Strouss, Hirshberg was a

German-born entrepreneur Isaac Strouss cut a dapper figure in the mid-1870s. *Courtesy of Mahoning Valley Historical Society.*

David Theobald's store in downtown Youngstown thrived in the late nineteenth century. Theobald served as a mentor to his cousin, Isaac Strouss, who later formed a business partnership with Bernard Hirshberg, another of Theobald's employees. *Courtesy of Mahoning Valley Historical Society.*

German-Jewish immigrant, but his circumstances were otherwise radically different.

Born in Hanover, Germany, in 1850, Hirshberg arrived in the United States with his family in 1862, when he was thirteen years old. His father, Jonas Hirshberg, had been a prosperous merchant in Germany, and young Bernard was apparently an outstanding student. His obituary indicated that, within six months of his arrival in the United States, "he was able to speak English fluently and had been promoted to the highest grade in the school."[33] Hirshberg spent the rest of his formative years in New Brighton, Pennsylvania, relocating to Youngstown at the age of eighteen after securing a position with David Theobald & Co. He evidently had varied interests, many of which did not involve commerce. Hirshberg was, for example, an accomplished violinist, with an impressive singing and speaking voice.[34] Even his business interests extended well beyond retail, and in later years Hirshberg became invested in the mining industry. In short, he appeared to lack the single-minded intensity of his future business partner, a difference that could help to explain their enduring friendship—one that Hirshberg later claimed "was never marred by an unkind word or act."[35]

Major developments leading up to the Strouss-Hirshberg business partnership included Theobald's announcement of his retirement from the retail sector and his offer to sell his interest in the Woolen Store to his young cousin. Isaac Strouss, in turn, presented Bernard Hirshberg with a proposal to jointly invest in the company. After the sale's conclusion, Theobald used his contacts to guarantee that the new business partners were able to secure adequate credit. As Strouss put it decades later, "It was [Theobald] who gave us good advice, much encouragement, and recommended us for credit with leading concerns in the eastern market, with the remark—'These boys are as good as the Bank of England.'"[36]

Interestingly, Theobald, for all his generosity, was not without his personal idiosyncrasies. In the early 1880s, when Ohio governor George Hoadley appointed him as one of his ten aides-de-camp, granting him the honorary title of "colonel," Theobald evidently took the title to heart. From that point on he was publicly referred to as "Colonel Theobald," and late in his life he was photographed wearing an elaborate uniform.[37]

Whatever his eccentricities, however, Theobald was a reliable advocate for his cousin, Isaac Strouss, and the bonds of affection between the two men were undoubtedly deepened in 1874, when Strouss married Lena Pfaezler, the sister of Theobald's son-in-law, Simon Pfaelzer. Their friendship remained strong until 1886, when Theobald died at the age of sixty-one. The pioneer retailer would be praised in the local media as "a straightforward, conscientious and upright citizen, with a hand and purse ever open for charity."[38]

Significantly, Strouss and Hirshberg's first store offered few hints of developments to

In the 1860s, Youngstown retailer David Theobald took seventeen-year-old immigrant Isaac Strouss under his wing and assisted in his rise as an entrepreneur. A pillar of the business community, Theobald also served as the first president of Temple Rodef Sholom, Youngstown's oldest Jewish congregation. *Courtesy of Mahoning Valley Historical Society.*

come. According to a newspaper article published decades later, the company "began business with the Woolen Goods store stock in a room 18 by 65 feet." The firm grew rapidly, however, and two years later, in 1877, the young retailers found themselves in need of more space and "moved into a room 26 by 80 feet." Then, in 1878, Strouss and Hirshberg found it necessary to build an addition to the existing store. During this period, the retailers' approach to sales bore little resemblance to the sophisticated strategies later employed at the Strouss-Hirshberg Department Store. "Goods were then unpacked on the sidewalk in front of the store," a later newspaper article observed. "Often merchandise was displayed on boxes on the sidewalk." The same article noted that the business partners "saved every board from packing cases" and used stencils to create signboards during the evening. "They would take the signs and place them along roads leading into Youngstown early in the morning," the article added. By 1887, the store had moved yet again, this time to the recently completed Wick Building, which still stands a block west of the city's Central Square.

Initially, the building's ground floor proved too large, and "[s]helves were often filled with empty boxes to keep up appearances." The business grew steadily, however, and by 1893 Strouss & Hirshberg had taken over the building's second and third floors. In time, the store's attractions included a hydraulic elevator, which the local media described as "the best between New York and Chicago."[39] "The store now occupied by the firm is the largest and handsomest occupied by any dry goods firm in the city," the *Vindicator* reported in April 1893. "The entire establishment is devoted entirely to… dry goods…and is divided into several departments, each stocked with a magnificent, varied and complete lines of goods." The article placed the store's floor space at "46 feet front and 150 feet deep" and noted that it retained seventy employees, "who have been selected for their knowledge of the articles they are called upon to sell, and who are at all times under requirement to afford courteous treatment and attention to customers."[40]

By 1893, a balding (albeit still trim) Isaac Strouss was one of the city's leading businessmen, and his successful professional life was complemented by a satisfactory home life. All accounts suggest that he was devoted to his wife, Lena, and their marriage would later be described as "a splendid example of sympathy, understanding and affection."[41] Their compatibility may have been enhanced by the fact that Isaac and Lena Strouss were both immigrants. In April 1893, when Lena's father, Max Pfaelzer, died at home in Kaiserslautern, Germany, the event may well have prompted Isaac to reflect on the distance separating him from his own European relatives.[42] Determined to start a family

This undated photograph of Lena Pfaelzer Strouss, wife of Isaac Strouss, captures her youthful beauty. The Philadelphia resident was the sister of David Theobald's son-in-law. *Courtesy of Mahoning Valley Historical Society.*

of their own, the couple had purchased a stately home on the city's north side, not far from the current site of Youngstown's Masonic Temple, and before long they had two children, Clarence and Helene.

His daughter Helene would eventually marry Youngstown attorney I. Harry Meyer, and in later years, their son, Jerold Meyer, would serve as director of the family firm. Clarence proved to be as industrious as his father, although his well-meaning curiosity occasionally got him into trouble. In 1890, the four-year-old Clarence alarmed his parents when he attempted to warm his bed by placing a lighted candle directly beneath it, a move that had predictable results.[43] By 1893, the boy was safely enrolled at the Wood Street Elementary School—five years later, at the age of twelve, he would become the youngest freshman at Youngstown's Rayen High School (popularly known as "The Rayen School"), which was located directly across the street from the Strouss family's home. In 1902, after his graduation from Mt. Pleasant Military Academy in Ossining, New York, Clarence Strouss was poised to become fully engaged in the family business.[44]

Young Clarence's involvement in the store overlapped with a period of dramatic expansion. In 1902, the partners announced they would initiate a $10,000 remodeling project destined to "alter the store completely, change

Strouss-Hirshberg Co. delivery trucks like the one pictured here braved violent weather and unpaved roads to provide service to customers in the early twentieth century. *Courtesy of Mahoning Valley Historical Society.*

and enlarge the various departments, etc." Two hundred and fifty feet of glass counters were ordered for the project, and plans were set to install display windows "of the newest and best pattern." To ensure that the project reflected the most recent innovations in the retail sector, a representative of the store was sent to study practices in retail hubs such as New York City. "The competent floor-walker, Mr. I.G. Goldsmith, recently returned from an eastern trip during which he made a careful study of the metropolitan stores, their plans, and the like, with a view to introducing some of the ideas there secured into the proposed change," the *Vindicator* reported in January 1902.[45]

Four years later, in 1906, the public learned of another major development as Bernard Hirshberg announced he would retire from active involvement in the firm. In late June, a report was issued that the partnership would be dissolved on July 1, 1906, a development owing mainly to Hirshberg's plans to "devote his time to mining business and other enterprises." The partners further announced that the "affairs of the partnership" would be managed by a corporation known as the Strouss-Hirshberg Co. "The name Strouss & Hirshberg has been a household one in Youngstown for years," the *Vindicator* reported. "No better praise is to be found than in the fact that the name will be retained in the corporation title of the business." This development did not signal Hirshberg's complete departure from the business, but it did create a vacuum in the firm's leadership that Clarence Strouss appeared willing, and able, to fill. "Clarence Strouss, who will be associated with his father in the new company, is one of the rising young business men of Youngstown," the *Vindicator* observed. "He has displayed wonderful executive ability since he entered the employ of the old firm and is ambitious, combinations that make for success in the business world today."[46]

In 1911, just four years after the firm's incorporation, the department store gained a larger home when the Strouss-Hirshberg Co. erected a six-story building on Commerce Street, directly behind the Wick Building. The project, which tripled the store's floor space, was completed by early 1912—just in time for the company's thirty-seventh anniversary. While the new building "was believed to have solved the question of space for many years," the firm was compelled to lease a portion of an adjacent building as early as 1914.[47] One year later, in 1915, the firm celebrated its fortieth anniversary in style at Youngstown's Ohio Hotel (later known as "the Pick-Ohio Hotel"), and the department store's expansion served as the event's organizing theme. "That the company has grown more than a few inches since it began is evident to everyone in Youngstown," the *Vindicator* observed, "but it will be particularly impressed on all those attending this evening."[48]

This undated photograph shows staff members of the Strouss-Hirshberg Co. at the Ohio Hotel. In 1915, the firm marked its fortieth anniversary in the hotel's ballroom. *Courtesy of Mahoning Valley Historical Society.*

This pattern of growth would continue for the remainder of the decade. Indeed, three years later, in 1918, the Strouss-Hirshberg Co. announced that it would embark on a building project that would leave the "heart of the business district…completely changed." As the *Vindicator* reported, "A 10 or 12 story million dollar building spreading itself from the First National bank on Federal street to the Wick building…will be built to house the Strouss-Hirshberg establishment." To pave the way for the new building, representatives of the firm negotiated a ninety-nine-year lease with the property's owners, who were reportedly "the heirs of the late Charles J. Wick and Hannah Wick," members of one of Youngstown's most prominent families.

According to the *Vindicator*, the $3 million deal involved "frontage of 119 feet on West Federal street, run[ning] 300 feet deep to Commerce street, extend[ing] 164 feet on Commerce street…and from that point, 190 feet on North Phelps to the Wick building." The paper noted that the lease was

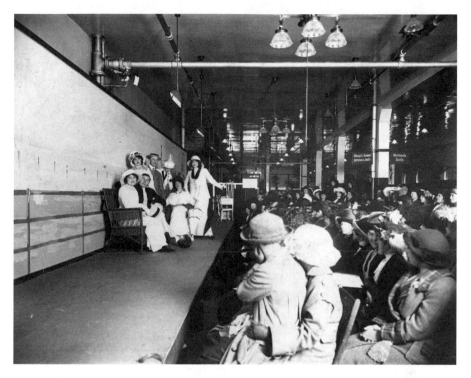

Over the years, fashion shows drew the public's attention to Strouss-Hirshberg's varied line of clothing. This undated photograph documents a show that was held in the 1910s. *Courtesy of Mahoning Valley Historical Society.*

effective on April 1, 1922, and pointed out that the project would displace dozens of businesses, including the confectionary of Youngstown businessman Harry Burt, who would later develop the famous Good Humor Bar at another downtown site.[49]

The firm's local expansion evidently spurred its exploration of overseas markets. In 1923, many local residents were surprised to learn of the extent of the Strouss-Hirshberg Co.'s involvement in the international textile trade, when local newspapers reported that the firm's office in Yokohama, Japan, was likely destroyed in an earthquake that leveled the city.[50]

Throughout this period, Youngstown's expansion closely paralleled the growth of the local steel industry, which had largely supplanted the burgeoning iron industry of the previous century. In 1901, local industrialists George D. Wick and James A. Campbell organized what became known as the Youngstown Sheet and Tube Co., which emerged as one of the nation's most important regional steel producers.[51]

Developments like these contributed to an explosive rise in population that benefited local commerce.

By the 1920s, Clarence Strouss was shouldering much of the responsibility for the firm's daily operation, and in 1924 he would be elected as president of the Strouss-Hirshberg Co. Although Isaac and Clarence Strouss were equally dedicated to the store's development, it is worth noting that they were, in many ways, different personalities. Isaac Strouss's demeanor was apparently informed by an old-world restraint, while Clarence Strouss possessed the confidence and panache of a New World entrepreneur. He was, among other things, a fearless public speaker, and he gained popularity in the business community for his humorous and often self-deprecating "ballads."

In November 1914, during the eighth annual banquet of the Youngstown Chamber of Commerce, held at the Ohio Hotel, Clarence Strouss introduced local industrialist Joseph G. Butler Jr. with a preamble that included the following passage:

> *To those who do not know me by way of explanation,*
> *Before I go too far along I make this allegation,*
> *So in case it does not meet with your entire approbation,*
> *For the few words I say here tonight I get no remuneration.*[52]

In February 1915, Clarence Strouss introduced Butler once again—this time at a banquet organized to mark the opening of Youngstown's St. Elizabeth's Hospital. In an account of the evening, the *Vindicator* reported that "Mr. Strouss already has come into fame as a bard after the fashion of the twelfth century when the deeds of valor among knights were sung by the ballad singers."[53] About five years earlier, in June 1910, Clarence Strouss had been the subject of a feature story on the challenges facing local equestrians after the paving of most of Youngstown's roads. "A few years ago, horseback riding was a favorite pastime," the article stated. "Then the automobile came in to replace it, and good roads also had their part in the banishment of the horse." In the article, Clarence Strouss was singled out for praise because he had fitted his favorite horse, Prince, with rubber shoes to minimize the discomfort of trotting on paved roads.[54]

For all their differences in temperament and style, however, Isaac and Clarence Strouss were both known for their approachability: a quality that apparently contributed to a corporate culture that employees—even decades later—would describe as "familial." Moreover, Clarence Strouss took deep

During the Strouss-Hirshberg Co.'s fiftieth anniversary, in 1925, decorations covered the façade of the store's third edifice. *Courtesy of Mahoning Valley Historical Society.*

pride in his father's accomplishments, an attitude reflected in his meticulous plans for the firm's golden jubilee. Indeed, given the anticipated scale of the celebration, it would have been impossible to stage the event in the elegant ballroom of the Ohio Hotel, which had been the venue for the fortieth-anniversary celebration.

A capacity crowd was on hand to celebrate Strouss-Hirshberg's fiftieth anniversary at downtown Youngstown's YMCA in 1925. *Courtesy of Mahoning Valley Historical Society*.

As it turned out, the hundreds of guests who arrived at the fiftieth-anniversary banquet on the evening of March 7, 1925, found they had little room to maneuver in the spacious gymnasium of Youngstown's YMCA. "With music and wit and a delicious spread, the assembly entered into the celebration like a happy family," the *Vindicator* reported on the morning after the event. "The founders beamed on the store personnel like proud fathers and every word they uttered was cheered lustily."[55]

The high point of the after-dinner program was the presentation of framed portraits of the founders. The portraits had been painted by Youngstown-born artist Edith Stevenson Wright, whose subjects ranged from U.S. president Calvin Coolidge to legendary actress Greta Garbo.[56] The portraits, it was announced, would hang on the main floor of the new, state-of-the-art Strouss-Hirshberg Department Store, whose construction was to begin in March of the following year.[57]

Visibly moved by the tribute, Isaac Strouss briefly took the podium and described the store's early history, reserving special praise for the late David Theobald and Youngstown banker Robert McCurdy, who had provided credit to the fledging enterprise in the late nineteenth century.[58] Isaac Strouss went on to compliment the store's leading executives: Clarence Strouss, Isaac Goldsmith and George Thompson.

This elegant window display marked the Strouss-Hirshberg Co.'s fiftieth anniversary. *Courtesy of Mahoning Valley Historical Society.*

When Hirshberg took his turn at the podium, he remarked on the challenges the store would likely face in the future, expressing confidence that the firm's leaders would meet them effectively. Hirshberg closed his remarks by commenting, "I hope to be present at the next anniversary." At that point, Isaac Goldsmith, the store's managing director, presented the partners with gold watches. "We are here to honor the successful rounding out of 50 years in business of two of Youngstown's leading merchants," Goldsmith announced to the crowd. "But in a larger and greater sense we are honoring the success in life and character of the founders."

Similar testimonials abounded, but the keynote address of the evening was delivered by Dr. I.E. Philo of Temple Rodef Sholom, who spoke on the topic "The Ideal of Service." "It is a rare thing—almost unprecedented in mercantile history—for two partners to live to round out 50 years of active service in a large enterprise," Dr. Philo observed at one point in his speech. "It is rare for two men to work together for half a century in fine friendship, spiritual understanding, and consecrated comradeship in the interest of the community."[59]

Less than four weeks later, Dr. Philo gravely surveyed the crowd that gathered in the auditorium of Temple Rodef Sholom to mark the passing of Isaac Strouss. The building was filled to capacity, a detail readily confirmed by local reporters. "For blocks around the Rodef Sholom Temple, cars of all descriptions were parked," the *Vindicator* reported. "Inside the doors of the Temple, men and women struggled for a place. Every seat in the edifice was occupied and those not fortunate enough to have been there early were compelled to stand in the rear."[60]

As the rabbi gazed out on the auditorium, his thoughts may have turned to a similar crowd that had gathered ten years earlier for the building's dedication. As a longtime trustee of the congregation, Isaac Strouss had been actively involved in that ceremony, and like others, he undoubtedly overheard members of the congregation as they compared the new edifice to its more elaborate predecessor. The old temple had been designed in what contemporary observers described as a "Moorish style," featuring large stained-glass windows and a domed turret. Upon its completion, the building's spire could be seen from several points in the city. The new temple, however, was notable for its "severity and plainness of design," an approach that was intended "to express the simplicity of the creed and the truth and dignity of the service it is to perpetuate."[61]

Fittingly enough, Dr. Philo's eulogy focused on what he described as the "simplicity" of the man whose memory they were to honor that afternoon. "If Isaac Strouss…could speak, he would, I am sure, not wish us to give utterance to any formal eulogy," Dr. Philo began. "He was a man who disliked ostentation, who loved simplicity."

After a short pause, the rabbi added, "Could he speak now he would voice the sentiment of Victor Hugo: 'My deeds must be my life, and when I am dead my actions must speak for me.'" As Dr. Philo continued, he highlighted Strouss's role as a civic leader who had "converted" his gifts "into the building of an enterprise honoring to God and helpful to man." Over time, the speaker said, Isaac Strouss had "called hundreds to help him build this enterprise, to share in the joy and glory of the adventure," and those participants "became his co-workers, members of his co-operating family, his comrades and friends." The rabbi went on to discuss the late businessman's kind disposition as well as his insistence on doing "his duty and a little more."

In his conclusion, Dr. Philo spoke emphatically: "It is the doing of our duty and a little more, that lifts life above the plane of mediocrity, that rescues it from the commonplace, that gives it the stamp of genius, that wins for it the

Isaac Strouss shares a relaxing moment with his grandson, Clarence Strouss Jr., in 1924.
Courtesy of Mahoning Valley Historical Society.

applause of men, that exalts it where a world gazes and wonders."[62] Although the rabbi's overview of his subject's varied accomplishments was undoubtedly heartfelt, it is not difficult to imagine that Dr. Philo was also saddened by the knowledge that Isaac Strouss had failed to witness the final ripening of the fruits of his labor. Ultimately, it would be left to his son, Clarence, to lead the enterprise to its next—and most spectacular—level of development.

CHAPTER 2

"A Metropolitan Enterprise"

On the evening of November 1, 1926, as the grand opening of the new Strouss-Hirshberg Department Store came to a close, Clarence J. Strouss must have looked back with satisfaction on the day's events. The store's grand opening had drawn the admiring attention of Youngstown's municipal leaders, and even representatives of Strouss-Hirshberg's most serious competitors in the local retail sector offered up words of praise. Given the event's overall success, it is easy to imagine Clarence Strouss leaning back in his chair, puffing on his ever-present pipe and envisioning a future that held still brighter prospects. This brand of optimism permeated the city's business sector at a time when Youngstown's continued growth appeared beyond question. Between 1900 and 1920, the city's population had more than tripled, rising from 44,885 to 132,358.[63]

Five years later, in October 1925, engineers at Ohio Bell Telephone Co. predicted that the city's population would approach 500,000 by 1950 if it continued to rise at its current rate.[64] At the time, the region's steel industry was booming, and the U.S. stock market was setting new records, with investors often paying as little as 10 percent in cash for stocks while banks financed the remainder for interest rates of 10 to 15 percent.[65] Buoyed by this prosperity, an unprecedentedly large youth generation was developing a culture marked by conspicuous consumption.

Given the circumstances, Clarence Strouss had every reason to believe he was leading an enterprise that was positioned to exploit opportunities that even his father, Isaac Strouss, couldn't have imagined. Yet, memories of the

An airplane hovers over the new Strouss-Hirshberg Department Store and its older neighbor, the Wick Building, in November 1926. The airplane dropped a floral tribute from the city's mayor as part of a ceremony to mark the facility's grand opening. *Courtesy of Mahoning Valley Historical Society.*

late retailer must have imbued the grand opening with a bittersweet quality, not only for his son, Clarence, but also for many others who were present. The *Vindicator* reported that, when elderly Bernard Hirshberg rose to discuss the store's early history, his "voice quivered and tears came to his eyes as he spoke of his partner…whose moment of supreme joy and happiness would have been realized had he been spared to witness the notable event that was being enacted."[66]

For the most part, however, the store's grand opening functioned as a daylong celebration of the future and a tribute to modern technology. The festivities had opened with the arrival of a biplane that swooped over West Federal Street and dropped a parachute into the center of Youngstown's retail district. The stunt hadn't come off precisely as planned, given that the parachute's cargo, a boxed wreath that the mayor intended to present to Strouss, became stranded on one of the new building's cornices.

The setback proved negligible, however, thanks to the intervention of company employee Paul Hammaker, who retrieved the box and placed it in the waiting hands of Youngstown's mayor, Charles Scheible. There were smiles all around as Mayor Scheible presented the wreath to a beaming

Clarence J. Strouss Sr. (right) accepts a wreath from Youngstown mayor Charles F. Scheible (left) to mark the $2.5 million department store's grand opening on November 2, 1926. The floral wreath was dropped by parachute from an airplane that circled the building three times. *Courtesy of Mahoning Valley Historical Society.*

Clarence Strouss, and both men held the pose for local photographers. Those who had gathered for the spectacle hadn't been disappointed, and onlookers were probably thrilled at the sight of an airplane circling the city's towers. It's unlikely that many of them had witnessed this kind of spectacle at such close range—and the surprises didn't end there. The newly constructed store was itself a monument to technological innovation, although such innovations were turned to the traditional task of improving customer service.

This was certainly true of one of the store's most interesting features, a one-hundred-station pneumatic tube service that provided almost immediate communication between the clerks on the floor and the cashier's station. To conclude a sale, all a clerk had to do was take payment, place it in a canister and send it via the pneumatic tube to the cashier. The cashier would then make change and send it back to the clerk. In cases where the transaction was a charge or a check, it was forwarded to the appropriate person for authorization and then promptly sent back to the clerk. This process allowed customers to use checks and charge accounts quickly and easily at the point of sale—a novel and practical use of this technology. Another innovation that came into play at the point of sale was the use of chutes at different points on the sales floors. This allowed the clerks to quickly transfer packages to the basement, where they were collected and sent to a substation on Wood Street a few blocks north of the department store. At that point, they were sorted and sent out for delivery. This made it possible for customers to continue their day of shopping without toting packages all over town. Innovations such as these would provide a pleasing, seamless experience for customers, and they also contributed to the department store's growing reputation for quality customer service.

Those who explored the building encountered many other examples of technology designed to ensure comfort and convenience. The structure contained five passenger elevators, each of which was attractively decorated with walnut trim. These elevators provided easy access to the four floors of sales items as well as the basement, where a soda fountain and cafeteria were located. Beyond the convenience of the elevators, customers could stop at one of the numerous water fountains installed throughout the store and sip water that was "chilled to the coolness of a mountain spring."

The machinery for the elevators—and for making the ice that chilled the water fountains—was housed in a twenty-five-thousand-square-foot penthouse on the building's roof. The refrigeration equipment was capable of producing one hundred tons of ice per day, which met the requirements not only for the water fountains but also for the soda fountain in the basement. The refrigeration unit also cooled the store's fur-storage vault—an amenity available to Strouss-Hirshberg's wealthier customers.

Along with the penthouse on the roof of the building were two twenty-five-thousand-gallon tanks of water that drew from the building's well and also from the city water lines. These tanks supplied water to the sprinkler system, which had three thousand heads distributed throughout the building, including within the store's display windows and fur-storage vault. In the event of a fire, the building and everything in it stood a very good chance of surviving with minimal damage. This elaborate state-of-the-art system suggests that Clarence Strouss and the company's other stakeholders intended for the store to operate at least as long as the ninety-nine-year lease, while also maintaining the Strouss-Hirshberg "family" of employees and customers.

Even the twenty-five-thousand-square-foot basement reflected the designers' preference for cutting-edge technology. To prevent mustiness, the area was ventilated in a way that facilitated a complete change of air every

Customers who walked through the West Federal Street exit, shown here as it appeared in the late 1920s, entered an arcade of display windows that featured the latest fashions. *Courtesy of Mahoning Valley Historical Society.*

three minutes. Therefore, visitors to the cafeteria or soda fountain were sure to find the air there as fresh as the air outdoors, if not a bit fresher.[67]

The department store's success, of course, did not depend entirely on technology. For decades, the firm had relied on a large staff of dedicated workers, many of whom treated their jobs as lifelong careers. About a year earlier, in March 1926, each of the store's 293 employees had signed a commemorative booklet printed to mark the Strouss-Hirshberg Co.'s fiftieth anniversary. Everyone connected to the store, including the founders, listed his or her birthday in the book, and all of them received a customized copy of the document.[68]

The management's attempt to create a familial environment was also reflected in the content of Strouss-Hirshberg's internal newsletter, *Store Stuff*, which featured humorous tidbits about managers and workers alike. Quotes from staff members ranged from memorable phrases to amusing malapropisms. In a newsletter circulated on March 13, 1926, almost eight months before the opening of the new store, company director Jerold Meyer

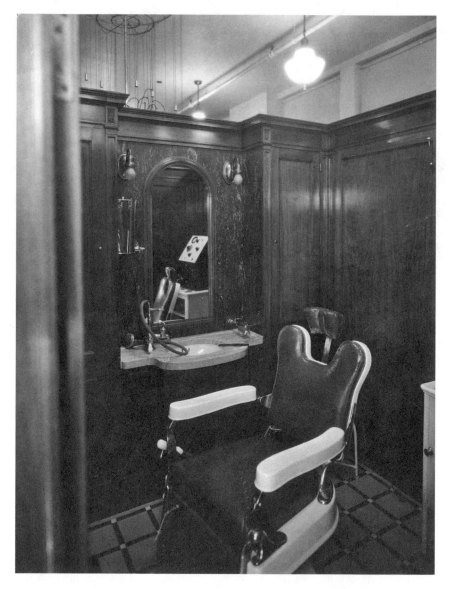

A full-service department store, Strouss' offered a broad range of amenities to customers. This undated photo, probably taken in the late 1920s, shows the store's barbershop. *Courtesy of Mahoning Valley Historical Society.*

was quoted as saying, "I'm going to provide my girls with lassoes—so they can rope more customers." Meanwhile, salesperson Maude Beatty, while struggling to slip into her galoshes, reportedly exclaimed, "Oh, I got this foot in the wrong sleeve!" Newsletters also encouraged employees to think beyond the needs of their own department. "An excellent way to make up for the lack of time is suggestive selling," one newsletter recommended. "If you suggest things in your own department, you make larger sales—if in other departments you are showing true S-H cooperation."[69]

Another factor in the boosting of employee morale was the introduction of policies and programs that reflected concern about workers' well-being. In January 1926, several months after Isaac Strouss's death, his two children, Clarence Strouss and Mrs. Helene Meyer, established the Isaac Strouss Memorial Foundation Fund, which was designed to assist any employee "in need of funds because of unfortunate circumstances."[70] Notably, this move was not entirely unprecedented. As far back as 1915, during the celebration of the firm's fortieth anniversary, managers had announced that the company "had arranged with the Equitable Life of New York for the purchase of group insurance on the lives of everyone of the store—from the youngest office boy and wrapping girl, to the president and general manager."[71] At the same time, the firm encouraged workers to purchase company stock, and by November 1926 it was reported that about 25 percent of employees were shareholders in the Strouss-Hirshberg Co. As the *Vindicator* stated, "This means that more than 100 who serve in various capacities—from delivery boy to president—have a very decided personal reason, beyond the remuneration that mere salary brings for being attentive to business."[72] During this period, employees also benefited from formal training that was overseen by Columbia University alumnus Goldie C. Conry, praised by the Ohio Department of Education "as a leader in inspiring others to a vision of true service."[73]

On July 5, 1928, less than two years after the store's grand opening, Clarence Strouss celebrated his twenty-fifth year of service with the Strouss-Hirshberg Co. The *Vindicator* noted that Strouss, who became officially connected with the store in 1903, was treated to a surprise luncheon held at the farm of his nephew, Jerold Meyer, in neighboring North Lima, Ohio. As the guests gathered on the lawn of Meyer's farmhouse, Bernard Hirshberg, the company's co-founder and first vice-president, offered a "glowing" tribute to Clarence Strouss. When Hirshberg finished his remarks, George V. Thompson, the firm's second vice-president, presented the young chief executive with "a beautiful testimonial, bearing the sentiments of his associates and containing a tinted photograph of himself and the new store front."[74]

At this time, Strouss had every reason to celebrate, given that his company was poised to expand beyond the borders of Ohio. On February 1, 1929,

Strouss-Hirshberg's store in New Castle, Pennsylvania, which opened in 1929, was its longest-operating branch. *Courtesy of Mahoning Valley Historical Society.*

less than six months after the anniversary luncheon, the Strouss-Hirshberg Co. established its first branch in Pontiac, Michigan, and one month later it opened a second branch in neighboring Flint, Michigan. Then, on September 14, 1929, the firm marked the grand opening of its third branch, in New Castle, Pennsylvania, which occupied the first three floors of the Frew Furniture Co. building. The *Vindicator* reported that the company spent more than $50,000 on "the new interior settings and fixtures, and for attractive show windows." Company director Jerold Meyer assumed management of the new store, assisted by Strouss-Hirshberg employee F.M. Cosby and Newcastle resident Gertrude Fulkerson.[75]

From a remove of more than eight decades, it is difficult to judge the scope of Clarence Strouss's plans for his company during the late summer of 1929. If Strouss envisioned his firm as a major player in the nation's retail sector, however, these plans would be compromised by the onset of the Great Depression, which threatened the company's very survival. The roots of the crisis can be traced, in part, to U.S. economic policies that emerged in the wake of World War I. During the consecutive administrations of Presidents Warren G. Harding and Calvin Coolidge, the U.S. government maintained exceptionally high tariffs on imports—a policy that led to a decrease in foreign trade and slowed the recovery of war-torn Europe. As undercapitalized European nations struggled to repay their war debts to the U.S. government, they borrowed from U.S. lending institutions, which, in turn, provided increasingly easy credit—especially under the Coolidge administration.

Yet, before the Wall Street crash of October 1929, few U.S. residents (outside of the beleaguered agricultural sector) were complaining. "However questionable the easy credit policies may have been—resulting in a growing burden of indebtedness and many uncollectable loans—they generated enormous prosperity in the U.S. and a semblance of it in Europe," noted David F. Burg, in his historical overview of the Great Depression. "Corporate net income in the United States surged from $8.3 billion in 1923 to $10.6 billion in 1928, a 28 percent increase."

Nor were corporations the only beneficiaries of the "Coolidge Prosperity." "Even industrial workers saw their earnings increase during these years by 8%, while the average work week shortened by nearly two hours to 45.7 hours," Burg explained. "The boom was enhanced by increased mechanization of production; cheaper electrical power; and new growth industries, such as automobiles, refrigerators, radios, movies."[76]

While the subsequent stock market collapse was an important turning point, it was also true that an already difficult situation was compounded in June 1930, when U.S. president Herbert Hoover signed into law the Hawley-Smoot Tariff Act, which produced the highest tariffs in U.S. history and effectively "strangled world trade."[77] "The worldwide circle of contention, uncertainty, retribution and protectionism between 1929 and 1933 helped produce a seemingly uncontrollable disintegration that defied comprehension, much less recovery," historian T.H. Watkins observed. "Calvin Coolidge, whose faith in the protocols of laissez-faire politics had been exemplary, contemplated the situation a few days before his death in January 1933 and told a reporter that even he had abandoned hope."[78]

By September 1930, the impact of the downturn was evident in Youngstown's steel sector, given that U.S. Steel, a major presence in the city's industrial core, had reduced the salaries of its remaining workers by 10 percent.[79] Such developments left a considerable percentage of Youngstown's population (now at its peak of 170,000) without adequate employment. In August 1931, local lawyer Benjamin Roth observed in his diary that

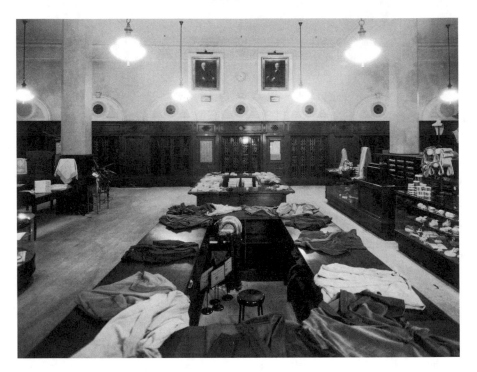

In the 1930s, women's fashion accessories were conveniently located near the store's elevators, which were staffed by uniformed operators. Portraits of Isaac Strouss and Bernard Hirshberg can be seen above the elevators. *Courtesy of Mahoning Valley Historical Society.*

prices had slipped drastically in the face of declining wages and growing unemployment. "It is almost unbelievable the ways prices have fallen in past two years," Roth observed. "Haircuts are now 25¢; shoe shine 5¢; a fairly good suit for men can be purchased for $25 (Strauss-Hirshberg [*sic*] has a window display at $9.90)."[80]

Three months earlier, in May 1931, the company dealt with another unsettling event, this time of a more personal nature. In the midst of what may have been the fifty-five-year-old firm's greatest crisis, its officers, directors and employees gathered to bid a final farewell to Bernard Hirshberg—perhaps the final link to the company's past. While long retired from active service, Hirshberg had been a benevolent (and highly symbolic) presence in the store until failing health prevented him from making his once daily visits.[81] According to his obituary, the former retailer had never fully recovered from an accident that had occurred two years earlier, when Hirshberg was struck by an automobile on Commerce Street, near the rear entrance of the Strauss-Hirshberg Department Store. Hirshberg's funeral

This undated photo (probably taken in the 1930s) of the street floor offers a view from the store's mezzanine. *Courtesy of Mahoning Valley Historical Society.*

service was held at Temple Rodef Sholom, where he had paid his final respects to his old friend Isaac Strouss just six years earlier.[82]

The advent of the Great Depression must have taken a serious toll on Clarence Strouss, coinciding as it did with a period of dramatic expansion for the Strouss-Hirshberg Co. In the wake of the downturn, the firm was apparently forced to sell its newly acquired branches in Michigan, although it was able to keep its new store in New Castle, Pennsylvania. Strouss probably found some comfort in his family life. By the summer of 1931, the chief executive and his wife, the former Elaine August, were raising four children: Clarence Jr., Sara, Albert and Stanley.

An interview Strouss gave to a *Vindicator* columnist, in July 1931, offered readers a rare glimpse into his personal life. The column noted that Strouss had maintained his passion for horseback riding ("Crawls out with the sun, on his horse by six"), which was matched by his devotion to his children ("Is 'a kid with the kids' and a great family man"). The Strouss family reportedly kept a summer cottage known as Claraine Woods (which combined the given

An official portrait of Clarence J. Strouss Sr. captures his warmth and approachability. Strouss served as president and general manager of the Strouss-Hirshberg Co. from the mid-1920s until his death in 1947. *Courtesy of Mahoning Valley Historical Society.*

names "Clarence" and "Elaine"), and Strouss maintained riding "trails all over Beaver Township." As an equestrian, he was frequently joined by his eldest son, Clarence Jr., then thirteen years old, who "[rode] with him most every morning."

While the column could be seen as a thumbnail sketch of a fun-loving family man, a closer reading suggests that Strouss's recreational activities were squeezed into a schedule that was generally quite hectic. The retailer acknowledged that he didn't play cards, rarely golfed and "[w]ould like to find time to read a few of the books in his extensive library." As things stood, he was forced "to be content with business and economic reading plus newspapers." Strouss also indicated he had taken "one vacation three years ago—a trip to the West Indies," although he had otherwise never been abroad.[83] The quality time he spent with family members, while precious, was seemingly a respite from a demanding schedule that revolved around the Strouss-Hirshberg Co.

Yet, business was not the only area of activity that demanded Strouss's attention outside the home. Like his father, Isaac, Clarence Strouss was a civic leader, and he was particularly involved in the affairs of Youngstown's growing Jewish community. By the 1930s, the local Jewish community bore scant resemblance to the small, informally organized group of mostly German and Austrian immigrants that Isaac Strouss had encountered back in the 1860s. These earlier settlers had been joined by immigrants from Russia, Poland, Lithuania, Hungary and Romania, who brought with them unfamiliar languages, different traditions and varying religious perspectives. Despite such differences, the Jewish community gradually integrated and went on to experience an extraordinary era of institution building. In 1893, less than a decade after the dedication of Temple Rodef Sholom, a community of mostly Hungarian Jews built a synagogue on Youngstown's north side to house the Orthodox congregation of the Children of Israel, which had been organized perhaps a decade earlier.[84]

Twelve years later, in 1905, a group of Polish and Russian Jews organized the Conservative congregation of Temple Emanu-El and eventually erected a brick building a couple of blocks to the northwest of Children of Israel.[85] In 1912, the same year members of Temple Emanu-El dedicated their new building, Hungarian and Lithuanian immigrants living on the city's east side organized what eventually became known as the Conservative congregation of Shaarei Torah.[86] Then, in 1919, the Conservative congregation of Anshe Emeth was organized by primarily Hungarian immigrants, who, in 1922, built an impressive temple in the fashionable north-side neighborhood surrounding Youngstown's Wick Park.[87] In 1920, the Orthodox congregation of Ohev Tzedak was organized on the south side, and in 1926, a permanent synagogue was dedicated.[88] Keeping pace with the rise of congregations was the explosive growth of social, political and service organizations.

In October 1930, when representatives of the Allied Jewish Campaign, a charitable organization, traveled from the East Coast to recruit a director

This 1930s photograph highlights the delicate ornamentation that remains an admired feature of the former Strouss' building. *Courtesy of Mahoning Valley Historical Society.*

for Youngstown's fundraising effort, they promptly scheduled a meeting with the president of the Strouss-Hirshberg Department Store, "for even in New York Mr. Strouss' influence among local Jewery [*sic*] is known." The *Vindicator* reported that the officials were "jubilant" when Strouss agreed to help raise $35,000 "and spent seven hours with him outlining plans for the most extensive campaign ever held here among the Jewish people."[89]

Perhaps Strouss's most enduring contribution to the local Jewish community, however, was his leadership role in the establishment of the Jewish Federation of Youngstown. The need to create some kind of "central community of organizations" arose, in part, from an explosion of relief organizations during the 1930s, many of which aimed to assist European Jews who were victims of organized anti-Semitism. After presiding over a meeting of twenty-six local Jewish leaders in August 1935, Strouss addressed a letter to the Jews of Youngstown, inviting them to meet on October 31, 1935, "to discuss the creation of a federated fund-raising mechanism."

Given the economic impact of the Depression, "there were fewer and fewer companies and individuals who could give," and the situation was compounded because "multiple new agencies were constantly being created for each and every worthy cause." This problem, Strouss proposed, could be resolved through the establishment of a federation "where all the money would be raised at one time, channeled through one agency and distributed to beneficiary agencies according to their rationally evaluated merit and need." The Jewish Federation of Youngstown came into being on October 31, 1935, with the approval of three sets of bylaws. The first meeting of the organization's board of directors took place a week later, on November 7, 1935, and before it was over, Strouss had been elected as the federation's first president.[90]

Under Strouss's leadership, the new organization established three departments—Family Welfare, Education and Social and Recreational—and by 1937, the federation had established offices in a former mansion located on Youngstown's north side; the structure also housed the city's first Jewish Community Center.[91]

Strouss's activities as a civic leader must have been difficult to balance with the task of maintaining a business during an economic depression, especially in the early 1930s. "Conditions get steadily worse and no relief in sight," wrote Youngstown-based lawyer Benjamin Roth in a January 28, 1933 journal entry. "For the third time in 2 years the employees of the Strouss-Hirshberg co. get a pay cut. This time 20%."[92] Drastic as such wage reductions might seem today, it is important to place them in the context of a period in which as many as 28 percent of U.S. households "did not have a single employed wage earner." Historian David E. Kyvig noted that, in 1933, "Americans overall had 54 percent as much income as in 1929," and "almost everyone knew of someone who had been rendered completely destitute."[93]

To ease the emotional pressures that accompanied "hard times," the Strouss-Hirshberg Co. used wage cuts to keep people "on the job," while

Armenian-born portraitist Mihran K. Seralian puts the final touches on a formal portrait of Clarence J. Strouss Sr. *Courtesy of Mahoning Valley Historical Society.*

also maintaining a corporate culture that offered employees numerous opportunities for social engagement. Company-sponsored outings to amusement parks and recreational centers in northeastern Ohio and western Pennsylvania continued throughout the 1930s, and the firm's executives often took an active role.

On August 16, 1936, during an employee picnic held at Myers Lake Park in Canton, Ohio, younger female workers participated in a "bathing beauty"

This 1930s photograph documents a typical family outing for Strouss-Hirshberg's employees. This picture may have been taken at Youngstown's Idora Park, a typical venue for such outings. *Courtesy of Mahoning Valley Historical Society.*

contest, while Strouss and the firm's general superintendent, George V. Thompson, engaged in a marshmallow-eating contest "in which charcoal-covered marshmallows were substituted for white ones on the blindfolded executives."[94] This sort of practical joke would hardly have taken place at a company-sponsored event at which most participants lived in fear of losing their jobs.

The incident also suggests that Clarence Strouss was a good-humored and approachable executive. "He was a great businessman who loved people, and who made certain that people—including customers and employees—were treated with respect," recalled C. Clark Hammit, who started working at the department store in 1933, when he was eighteen years old. Hammit indicated his first job was "reading" the store's forty-six cash registers, which involved reviewing tickets for each department and then each salesperson. In the mid-1930s, when Strouss learned that Hammit planned to attend Ohio State University, he asked him to help his son, Clarence Jr., in "getting started" at the university. "This was a good thing for me," Hammit recalled, "because I had transportation to Columbus." He noted that Clarence Strouss Jr. often allowed him to drive his DeSoto from Youngstown to Columbus.[95]

As the decade came to a close, the economy began to show signs of stabilizing. Following the Wall Street Crash, the U.S. economy had hit bottom during the winter of 1932–33. Then followed four years of very rapid growth until 1937, when there was another economic downturn that began in the middle of the year and continued through 1938. This trend was reflected in a 1938 report to shareholders issued by Clarence Strouss. "The volume of sales [for 1937] for the first nine months showed a substantial increase over the corresponding period of 1936," the report stated. "In the last quarter, however, the industrial recession in the valley curtailed the spending power of our customers and quite naturally resulted in receding sales, which condition was and continues to be reflected in retail trade thruout [*sic*] the country."

In the end, though, the company nevertheless showed a net profit of $250,044.19 for 1937 and paid cash dividends of 97½ cents per share, which allowed Strouss to confidently claim that "the Company was in good financial position and is prepared to move forward when the uptrend is resumed." In the same report, Strouss announced that a new addition to the store was open for business:

> *The new addition to our building facing on Phelps Street has been completed. The luncheonette formerly located in the basement was moved to the first floor of the new addition and has met with the hearty approval of the public. On the mezzanine floor of the new addition a cafeteria and suitable rest rooms have been provided for our co-workers. The beauty parlor was moved to the second floor of the new addition during the early part of March, 1938.*

The only sour note in the otherwise positive report was an expression of concern about rising taxes: "Taxes figured importantly in the result of the year's operations and the earnings per share, and are the cause of growing concern not only to your management but to business in general." Total taxes had amounted to $162,032.74, "an increase of 29% over taxes for 1936 and increase of 100% over 1935."[96]

Positive trends within the domestic economy, however, were offset by troubling social and political developments—both at home and abroad. Anti-Semitism, which had surfaced briefly (albeit virulently) in the 1920s, made a powerful comeback in the 1930s with the rise of populist leaders such as Gerald P.

Well-dressed shoppers and pedestrians go about their business near Strouss-Hirshberg's elegant West Federal Street entrance in the late 1930s. *Courtesy of Mahoning Valley Historical Society.*

Winrod, William Dudley Pelley and Father Charles E. Coughlin, a Canadian-born priest whose radio show promoted anti-Jewish ideas.[97] As historian Eric L. Goldstein noted, anti-Semitism in the United States was closely related to the rise of Nazi Germany and the growing likelihood of an international conflict. This was especially true "after 1939, when conservatives pointed to Jewish influence as the force pushing the Roosevelt Administration toward war in Europe."[98]

Indeed, the scope of the threat posed by the Nazi-dominated Axis Powers would not become apparent to most Americans until December 7, 1941, when the Imperial Japanese Navy attacked the U.S. naval base at Pearl Harbor, a development that enabled "the Roosevelt Administration...to move vigorously against right-wing extremists, to brand them as Nazi agents, and hence as traitors."[99]

By that time, Clarence J. Strouss Jr. had already been enlisted in the U.S. Army for two years. Whether or not his decision to enlist had been motivated by reports of the Nazis' anti-Semitic activities remains unclear, but members of the Strouss family were surely aware of these developments, and some relatives were apparently troubled by the fact that their ancestral homeland had become the staging ground for an unprecedentedly vicious assault on European Jewry.

Strouss-Hirshberg's West Federal Street entrance featured an arcade of window displays, replete with vaulted ceilings and neo-Gothic hanging lights. In the 1960s, the arcade was demolished to make way for additional retail space. *Courtesy of Mahoning Valley Historical Society.*

On July 1, 1939, Clarence Strouss Sr. received a family heirloom from his cousin, Fred Kahn, who enclosed a letter that eloquently (if indirectly) expressed his deep misgivings about developments in Germany. The heirloom in question was a pocket watch that had once belonged to their common grandfather, the late Max Pfaelzer, who had lived in Germany. "As a member of the Pfaelzer family I bring this watch back, to this, the land of freedom and justice," Kahn's letter stated. "This watch is witness of wary [sic] trying times, but was always in honor. Not hunger, nor cold, nor persecution endangered the proud honor of this watch."[100]

With America's official entry into World War II, the Strouss-Hirshberg Co. publicly commended employees who had volunteered for military service (a group that included Clarence Strouss Jr.) and actively promoted the sale of war bonds at its flagship store and various branches. Buoyed by a wartime economy, the Strouss-Hirshberg Co. continued to see its profits grow, and the annual report to shareholders for 1944 earnings claimed a net profit (after taxes) of $467,428.79, compared to $401,669.23 for the previous year. Clarence Strouss Sr. noted that earnings per share were $2.53, compared with $2.17 the year before.

Meanwhile, the business began to expand at a rate not seen since the 1920s. Although steel products were unavailable for the construction of new stores due to wartime building restrictions, the Strouss-Hirshberg Co. was able to purchase Griswold's, a department store in neighboring Warren, Ohio. The store sold mainly home wares, a focus that the Strouss-Hirshberg Co. chose to continue, given that it complemented another branch the company had acquired in Warren in September 1940 that featured principally ready-to-wear clothes and accessories.

Even as Strouss assured shareholders that the business would continue to move forward, he took time to credit the sacrifices of the almost one hundred Strouss-Hirshberg employees (a quarter of the total staff) who had joined the country's fighting forces in various parts of the world. He went on to observe that those employees who remained behind "made enviable records in the sale of bonds, Red Cross, Community War Chest, and other war related activities."[101]

By the time the Allies declared victory in Europe and the Pacific, the Strouss-Hirshberg Co. was well positioned to compete in a postwar market. Net profits had risen to $566,911.79, up $98,483 from the previous year, and in typical fashion, Clarence Strouss Sr. cited the nation's success as a prime factor: "At this time we should acknowledge that increased national income, which was shared in our trading area, was the greatest single contributing factor to our successful operations." Furthermore, in the shareholder report of 1946, he again reminded shareholders of the sacrifices made by those Strouss-Hirshberg employees who had served overseas: "All but 23 of our service men and women have already returned, and we welcome them with deep and genuine appreciation of their war service."

War bond promotions were common at all of Strouss-Hirshberg's branches during World War II. This drive was held at the Sharon, Pennsylvania location in 1945. *Courtesy of Mahoning Valley Historical Society.*

He went on to commend store employees for their efforts during this same period: "We are mindful that much credit for our improvement over previous years was due to the efforts of our co-workers who maintained a high degree of loyalty and cooperation, thus enabling us to produce far better than average results."[102] Like his father, Isaac, Clarence Strouss Sr. evidently viewed the firm's success as a shared effort.

Given that the close of the war had brought with it a winding down of building restrictions, the Strouss-Hirshberg Co. was free to expand its retail sites, and the firm also planned extensive additions and alterations to the main store in downtown Youngstown. These plans included the razing of a building on Phelps Street, which ran along the store's western entrance, to make way for a new structure that would dramatically increase space on the main floor while also allowing for the installation of escalators.

Meanwhile, a retail site was acquired on Market Street, a commercial hub on the city's south side, and plans were made to connect a new building

This 1945 photograph of Strouss-Hirshberg's men's furnishings department, which was located on the street floor, features a display of men's ties that sold for fifty-five cents each. *Courtesy of Mahoning Valley Historical Society.*

with an existing one. This expanded structure would become the south-side branch of the department store's household appliance department. The company's directors also planned to build another structure on Wood Street, adjacent to an existing warehouse, to provide additional space for warehousing and service facilities.

Nor were the firm's plans for expansion limited to Youngstown itself. In his report to shareholders, Strouss noted that the company had purchased real estate in New Castle, which they planned to remodel and adapt to their existing store.[103] At long last, it seemed possible to realize Clarence Strouss Sr.'s long-standing dream to turn the Strouss-Hirshberg Co. into a major force within the region's retail industry. Sadly, however, the enterprise's final stage of development would have to wait until after Strouss's untimely death.

CHAPTER 3

Postwar Boom

When C. Clark Hammit strolled into the Strouss-Hirshberg Department Store in 1946, Clarence J. Strouss Sr., the company's president and general manager, may not have recognized him immediately. Some years had passed since their last meeting, and Hammit was no longer the wiry youth who Strouss had hired back in the 1930s. Tall and elegantly slim, he sported a stylish mustache and projected an air of quiet self-assurance. By this time, Hammit had two years of executive experience, and his career had taken him to major cities like Chicago and New York. In addition, between 1942 and 1945, he had served with distinction as a U.S. naval officer in the South Pacific. When the war ended, however, Hammit had felt "the tug of home," and when he mentioned his interest in returning to Youngstown, Strouss urged the young man to speak to the store's general superintendent, George V. Thompson, about a job.[104]

The gesture was typical. As a former employee, Hammit was regarded as a member of the Strouss "family" of workers, and while the Strouss-Hirshberg Co. occasionally hired talented executives who had no previous relationship with the firm, there was a marked preference for recruiting current or former employees for management positions. George Thompson was himself a beneficiary of this policy. In 1907, Thompson began working for the firm as a floorwalker and quickly rose up the ladder to become a buyer, assistant manager and general superintendent. Before his retirement in 1951, Thompson would serve as director, vice-president and president.[105]

An undated aerial photograph of downtown Youngstown calls attention to the Strouss-Hirshberg Co.'s prime location. The store, visible on the left side of the photograph, sits just west of the city's Federal Square. *Courtesy of Mahoning Valley Historical Society.*

Over time, Hammit's career would follow a similar trajectory, as he moved from a position at the New Castle store to a job as assistant general manager and then to general manager. Before his retirement in the 1980s, he would also serve as vice-president and general merchandising manager.[106]

Customers swarmed Strouss-Hirshberg's basement during "Remnant Day" specials like this one in 1949. *Courtesy of Mahoning Valley Historical Society.*

Clarence Strouss's loyalty to employees was generally reciprocated, and those who worked for him undoubtedly appreciated a corporate culture that fostered attitudes of mutual respect between managers and employees. It was the kind of atmosphere his father, Isaac Strouss, had insisted upon, and in certain ways, it resembled the environment of Clarence Strouss's own household.

Back in March 1941, when Clarence Jr., then serving as a lieutenant in the U.S. Army, abruptly announced plans to marry, his father's written response was devoid of criticism, let alone angry threats. The older man acknowledged that his reservations about the news stemmed, in part, from his own reluctance "to face the fact…that I am the father of a son of marriageable age." The retailer added, however, that he was also concerned about his son's failure to discuss the subject with him earlier. "We have ridden the trails together and there have been no subjects we could not discuss no matter how important nor how trivial," Clarence

Strouss Sr. had written. "It is because of this that I feel somewhat hurt; that you have apparently not felt like taking your Dad into your confidence on a matter of such great importance."

Clarence Sr. went on to advise his son about the risks of marrying young (Clarence Jr. was then about twenty-three years old) and also pointed to the uncertainty of the times. "If Hitler wins the war he will attempt to do on this continent what he has already done in Europe," the older man wrote. "You certainly are not unaware that his agents have been and are still spreading vicious anti-Semitic propaganda through the United States with the definite purpose in mind of dividing this country through racial hatred." In the letter's conclusion, Clarence Sr. requested a meeting to "sit down and talk this over."[107]

Although it is unclear whether such a meeting ever took place, it seems significant that Clarence Strouss Jr. preserved his father's letter. Furthermore, there is no evidence that the older man opposed his son's final decision, and Clarence Strouss Jr. married his former university classmate, Margaret Emmons, in April 1941. At home and at work, Clarence Strouss Sr. evidently preferred dialogue to confrontation.

Located a few blocks north of Youngstown's Central Square, the Strouss-Hirshberg Music Center catered to local musicians and served as a venue for music lessons and recitals. *Courtesy of Mahoning Valley Historical Society.*

While young men like Clark Hammit may have found the company's quasi-familial environment appealing, there were other attractions as well. The Strouss-Hirshberg Co., after an extended period of slow growth (due to the Great Depression and World War II), was once again an expanding enterprise. The downtown store, now eight stories high, offered customers the kind of shopping experience that most people associated with a larger metropolitan area. The store's new Phelps Street annex had not only paved the way for the installation of two state-of-the-art Westinghouse escalators, but it also added five thousand square feet of selling space to each floor. In addition, the store's luncheonette, which had been relocated in 1938 from the basement to the corner of Phelps and Commerce streets, emerged in the postwar era as one of the downtown's most popular eateries.

Meanwhile, a building that the firm had acquired on Wick Avenue (a few paces from the former site of Clarence Strouss's childhood home) had been refurbished and reopened as the Strouss-Hirshberg Music Center. The facility not only offered an impressive array of musical instruments, but it also served as a popular site of music lessons and recitals. By the winter of 1946, the company was preparing to open its South Side Appliance Shop on Market Street, and it had already undertaken the remodeling of its two branches in Warren, Ohio, and upgraded its oldest existing branch in New Castle, Pennsylvania.[108] All of these developments coincided with a postwar population explosion and economic boom, which injected new life into urban retail districts.

Many area residents believed that downtown Youngstown had never been more vibrant. Josephine Houser, a college student in the late 1940s and early 1950s, recalled that, while the district was crowded, social etiquette usually prevailed. "Back then, you could barely walk on the sidewalks, and stores were not open forever," she said. "But…people respected [others] and walked to the right one way, and walked to the left in the other lane."[109] This kind of population density was expected, given that the downtown was a center of retail, entertainment and government.

Furthermore, many of the city's leading medical professionals maintained offices in the district's tower buildings. "That was…one of the best parts of my life, working in the downtown," said Amelia Marinelli, who was employed at an ophthalmologist's office. Mrs. Marinelli added that, when she ventured downtown during working hours, she dressed formally and "even put my furs on," because the trip often involved a film at one of the district's movie palaces and dinner at an elegant restaurant.[110]

Interestingly, James Doran, who had relocated from nearby Cleveland as a child, was first struck by the modest size of the district, although

Three Lariccia sisters—Philomena (Vargo), Antoinette (Cafaro) and Concetta—pose for the camera during a 1950s stroll outside Strouss' Federal Street entrance. *Courtesy of Concetta Lariccia.*

he came to appreciate it "because [he] knew most of the action was on Federal Street."[111] Mary Ann Senediak also commented on the downtown's concentrated nature. "Everything centered on the downtown area," she recalled. "And when you shopped in the downtown area...you were

This 1954 photograph of Strouss-Hirshberg's women's hat bar located on the street floor conveys something of the store's elegant atmosphere. *Courtesy of Mahoning Valley Historical Society.*

dressed appropriately, professionally, as if you were going to church. You made it…a dining experience as well as a shopping experience—and a social experience, whether you were eating at the counter in Woolworth's or at the counter in Strouss'."[112]

For those who encountered this vibrant district as children, its effect was almost magical. "With Livingston's [Department Store], you walked in and there was perfumed air, and you felt very elegant and very ladylike shopping in that particular store," said Patricia Sveth, as she recalled trips to the downtown area with her mother. "And at Lustig's [Shoe Store]… my mom would shop in the salon upstairs…with large windows and pretty, overstuffed chairs and couches." On special occasions, Ms. Sveth noted, she would don a hat and gloves and dine with her mother at the Mural Room, an elegant restaurant located near the offices of the *Vindicator*, the city's daily newspaper. "I can remember…feeling very, very special," she said.

The Strouss-Hirshberg Department Store, in many ways, functioned as the centerpiece of this bustling hub. Children who visited the store savored the "adventure" of riding the elevators, whose uniformed operators occasionally made mistakes that resulted in a bumpy arrival at one's desired destination. The store's escalators were yet another attraction, and many children lingered on the store's mezzanine, which offered a dramatic view of the main floor.

The mezzanine's novelty shops, including a bookstore and camera department, inspired many youngsters to develop hobbies, including stamp and coin collecting, reading and even photography. "The bookstore…had an excellent selection of hardback and then, later, paperback books," recalled former resident Ben Lariccia, who "got started coin collecting" during visits to the mezzanine. One afternoon, the youth discovered that the stamp and coin shop was offering a discount on a Roman coin dating back to the first century, BCE. "In fact, it was the most common coin in the Roman Empire," he noted. "It wasn't expensive." Therefore, when his mother treated the item as an unnecessary expense, he took the news badly. "I came home and I threw a fit: 'I want that coin! I want that coin!'" he recalled, adding, "I got the coin." Lariccia noted that he still owns the coin—the first acquisition in what became a lifelong hobby of collecting.

Yet, for many young visitors, including Lariccia, the store's basement was a primary destination. Among the attractions found there was the

Strouss-Hirshberg's ushered in the spring with this "Tulip Time" window display, which appeared in the early 1950s. *Courtesy of Mahoning Valley Historical Society.*

children's shoe department, which featured a small X-ray machine that supposedly helped salespeople determine whether a pair of shoes was a proper fit. "You would see a kind of fluoroscope image of your bones inside the shoe," Lariccia recalled, noting that the machine often served as "the dealmaker." If a disagreement arose over whether the shoes fit, he added, the salesman would insist, "Let's take a look, with true science, with true science."[113] This "true science" was later exposed as faulty, even dangerous, but for children of the era, the fluoroscope was part of the drama they expected in a retail environment.

The most powerful lure of the basement, however, was a small counter located near the budget store. Reverend Deacon John C. Harris, a local financial manager, recalled that his mother's shopping marathons downtown always concluded at the snack bar in Strouss-Hirshberg's basement, which specialized in two items: Coney Island hot dogs and the store's famous chocolate malts. "That was the best," Reverend Harris said. "And the Strouss' malt came in a skinny glass...with a tall stem, and that was the reward for behaving during one of these long shopping trips."[114] Lariccia, who also recalled receiving malts for good behavior, described it as "the most incredible concoction," adding that it was "a super-light chocolate mousse."[115]

Holiday window displays such as this one, which appeared in 1952, created vivid memories for downtown visitors, especially children. *Courtesy of Mahoning Valley Historical Society.*

Likewise, Sally Absalom, a high school student during the 1940s, indicated she has never tasted anything that compares to the malts since the store's closing in the 1980s. "Other people say they have the recipe and that, but I've tried every one of them, and none of them are exactly the same," she said.[116]

This didn't surprise Richard Scarcella, a local educator and public historian, who insisted that the malt featured a "secret ingredient" that can no longer be used in commercial foods in the state of Ohio. "It was raw egg whites," Scarcella contended. "I guess, maybe, the chickens were cleaner years ago, because, today, egg whites have to be…standardized, pasteurized." He added that, while the original malt machine surfaces now and then at local fairs and festivals, the product "tastes nothing like the original."[117] Apparently, pasteurized egg whites do not produce the fluffy consistency and unique taste that people still associate with the Strouss' malt.

Youngstown residents of all ages were especially drawn to the downtown area during the holiday season, when the district was festooned with lights, bows, wreaths, holly and other decorations. The effect was probably amplified by the fact that few people decorated their homes' exteriors at the time. "This was probably the only area that had Christmas lights," Lariccia

Customers who entered Strouss-Hirshberg's West Federal Street arcade in December 1952 encountered this stylish nativity scene. *Courtesy of Mahoning Valley Historical Society.*

recalled. "We didn't see that in the neighborhoods. It wasn't until the late '60s that I remember seeing people spending lots of money to light up their homes."[118]

Apart from the decorations, shoppers encountered dynamic window displays, many of which featured mechanized figures, and it was widely believed that Strouss-Hirshberg's and McKelvey's department stores competed with each other to produce the most elaborate displays. The festive atmosphere was enhanced by the presence of holiday shoppers and seasonal music. "At Christmastime, it was very special, because there was just something about being outside—the people with their packages," said Reverend Harris, recalling his childhood excursions downtown. "And one thing that I really liked…was, at every hour the chimes would ring on the Home Savings & Loan building." He noted that, during the holidays, the chimes played Christmas music. "And how appropriate, to be walking down Federal Street in the winter, with all the Christmas decorations, and the Home Savings & Loan building starts to play, 'It's Christmas Time in the City'—[from] 'Silver Bells,'" he added.[119]

The transformation of the downtown retail district, of course, was hardly a spontaneous response to the holidays. Richard Scarsella, who was born into a local merchant family, explained that the decorating of the district was coordinated by an organization known as the Downtown Board of Trade. "Different stores would pool money and resources, and they would decorate Federal Street," he said. "So, it made downtown very welcoming. In fact, you would be able to hear music out on the sidewalks, along with the Salvation Army [hand] bells."[120]

Clarence Strouss Sr., as a leading member of the Downtown Board of Trade, was deeply involved in the district's annual transformation. An observant Jew and a prominent leader within his own religious community, Strouss was instinctively drawn to the Christmas season's humanitarian message. For years, he had played Santa Claus at Youngstown's Glenwood Children's Home, "going personally and taking a gift which he had selected himself for every child."[121] His civic activities made him a familiar and widely respected figure in the community at large, but the relentless pace of his schedule posed serious risks to his health. According to Strouss's obituary, he had been warned repeatedly to reduce his activities "but felt that his duties needed him and declined to take the rest he required."

On February 27, 1947, Strouss suffered a massive stroke while working in the downtown store. He was rushed to the north-side unit of the Youngtown Hospital Association, where he died several days later on March 7. Strouss

The cooperation of downtown merchants ensured that the holiday season would be memorable for local shoppers. In this 1955 photograph, Strouss' employees Dorothy Wigfall Green and Boyd Sellers sing "Silent Night" at a Christmas pageant. *Courtesy of Mahoning Valley Historical Society.*

was sixty years old. His passing sent shock waves throughout the community, and the *Vindicator* printed a front-page story with a banner headline announcing the tragedy. Significantly, Strouss's funeral service at Temple Rodef Sholom, which was led by Rabbi Dr. Sidney M. Berkowitz on March

Youngstown's Jewish Community Center, which opened to the public in 1954, was dedicated to the memory of Clarence J. Strouss Sr., who tirelessly promoted its establishment in the years before his death. *Courtesy of Mahoning Valley Historical Society.*

10, drew the participation of Dr. I.E. Philo, rabbi emeritus of the temple; Reverend Roland A. Luhman, pastor of First Reformed Church; and Dr. Russell J. Humbert, pastor of Trinity Methodist Church.[122] This interfaith gathering of religious leaders attested to the fact that Strouss's reputation had transcended ethnic and religious boundaries.

Four days after the funeral service, on March 14, the *Youngstown Jewish Times* printed an editorial that praised Strouss for his extraordinary contributions to the community. "Seldom in the history of the city of Youngstown did such a wave of sentiment sweep through the town as after the news of the death of Clarence J. Strouss came from the radios and from the newspapers," the editorial stated. "In the history of Youngstown there was seldom such a man as Clarence J. Strouss." The editorial added that, while Youngstown had suffered the loss of "a great civic leader," the local Jewish community had "lost its best and most widely known member."[123]

Less than three months later, on June 2, 1947, Paul B. Davies of the Mahoning Saddle and Bridle Association presented a eulogy that identified Strouss as perhaps the community's most substantial civic leader. "Many organizations of our city like the Mahoning Saddle and Bridle Association

Housed in a nineteenth-century landmark, Strouss-Hirshberg's Salem, Ohio store opened in 1948. *Courtesy of Mahoning Valley Historical Society.*

will miss the influence of Clarence Strouss in the days to come," Davies said. "Am I making the point too strong when I say that Youngstown has suffered the loss of its number one citizen? I think not."[124]

After Strouss's passing, George V. Thompson briefly assumed presidency of the firm. Less than a year later, on March 5, 1948, the public learned of yet another development affecting the store: the $5.7 million merger of the Strouss-Hirshberg department stores with the May Co., "on an exchange of stock transaction." Thompson, along with Morton May, president of the May Co., observed in a public statement that "directors of both concerns have recommended their shareholders approve the transaction."

According to the terms of the merger, the Strouss-Hirshberg Co. would receive 148,000 shares of the May Co.'s stock, valued at thirty-eight dollars a share on the New York Stock Exchange, in return for all of its assets. "May Co., in addition, will assume all liabilities of Strouss-Hirshberg," the *Vindicator* reported. "About 500 Strouss shareholders will get eight-tenths of a share of May Co. stock for each share of their

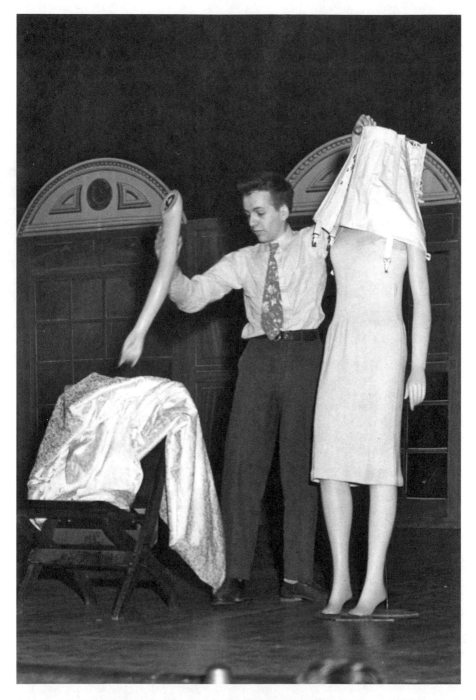

Strouss-Hirshberg window dressers, under the direction of display manager Earl Black, took tremendous pride in their work. This employee dresses a mannequin in preparation for a new display. *Courtesy of Mahoning Valley Historical Society*.

own," the paper added, noting that the firm's stock had been recorded at twenty-six dollars a share.

The merger was treated in the article as a fait accompli, given that "directors, officers and principal shareholders representing more than two-thirds [of] the outstanding stock already have assented." Interestingly, May contended that the Strouss-Hirshberg Co. (now treated as a division of the May Co.) would "continue its business under its own name, with the same management, policies and personnel," an approach that was consistent with the corporation's "policy of having its stores locally managed to remain an integral part of the communities they serve." Thompson also took pains to assure the public that the enterprise would not "lose its identity through the merger," and if anything, the move would strengthen "its position…to that of seven other big stores in the May group," including Pittsburgh-based Kaufman's, Akron-based O'Neill's and the May Co. stores in the Cleveland area.[125]

Perhaps the success of this strategy is reflected in the fact that many area residents continued to regard the Strouss-Hirshberg Co. (or Strouss', as it became known) as a locally owned enterprise. This perception would survive until the fateful merger of the Strouss' and Kaufman's Divisions in the 1980s. In any case, the terms of the merger were finalized at a special meeting of stockholders held at the store on the morning of March 29, 1948. It is worth mentioning that a notice of the meeting had been signed by Clarence J. Strouss Jr., then serving as secretary of the company's board of directors.[126] Less than four months later, on July 3, 1948, Strouss was informed in a letter of his election as an assistant secretary of the May Co.[127]

About sixteen months later, on November 11, 1949, Strouss-Hirshberg's internal newsletter, *Store Stuff*, announced that Clarence Strouss Jr. planned to leave the store on January 1, 1950, "in order to go into the business of tax analysis and estate planning" with the Northwestern Mutual Life Insurance Company.[128] This was by no means an obvious move, given that Strouss would be required to secure a strong background in an unrelated field. "He went at it the hard way," the *Vindicator* reported more than six years later, in March 1956. The paper noted that Strouss, already a graduate of Ohio State University, took "special courses" at Northwestern Mutual and also went on to secure credentials in life insurance marketing at Purdue University. "It is typical of Strouss and in the family tradition to do thoroughly anything he decides to work on," the *Vindicator* stated, admiringly.[129]

Although Clarence Strouss Jr. went on to became a successful businessman and civic leader in his own right, his departure from the Strouss-Hirshberg Co. marked the end of the family's involvement in

After the department store's merger with the May Co. in 1948, Clarence J. Strouss Jr. was elected as assistant secretary of the firm. In 1956, however, he made the bold decision to leave the firm and build a new, highly successful career in the field of insurance. *Courtesy of Mahoning Valley Historical Society*.

the firm's leadership. It is true that his younger brother, Stanley Strouss, remained connected to the store for years to come, but he served as a manager and salesperson, not as an officer or director.

Otherwise, however, the firm remained much the same—in line with the predictions of Morton May and George Thompson. Those who entered the store continued to receive the high levels of customer service that were an integral part of the Strouss-Hirshberg tradition. Indeed, customers of the period describe what they call a "personalized" shopping experience.

In the days before automated answering services, switchboard operators such as these played a vital role in delivering customer service. *Courtesy of Mahoning Valley Historical Society.*

"Customer service was unbelievable," recalled Josephine Houser. "You would walk up to a case that held sweaters, and the woman would say, 'May I help you?' And you would say, 'I'd like see that blue sweater in a size so-and-so.'" Mrs. Houser added, "She would take it out, open it for you, ask if you had any questions, [tell] you about washing instructions, if there were [any]."[130] In short, a single salesperson would take the customer through each step of the process, from the initial greeting to the final checkout.

Similarly, Betty Swanson, who worked at the adjacent Union National Bank in the 1950s, described the specialized service that she received at Strouss-Hirshberg's bookstore. "I am a reader and went to the book department a great deal," Mrs. Swanson recalled. "There was a lady there who knew of my interests, and she would save books for me when they went on sale. She was very, very kind."[131]

Richard Scarsella, a frequent shopper at the store, affirmed these observations. "In the olden days…the commissioned salespeople kept a file on their good customers," Scarsella said. "They would call you ahead of time and let you know that there was a sale; and what they would do, they would hold something back for you, maybe the day before the sale—and then, when the sale came the following day, you had all day to get downtown to pick up the item that they [kept] for you, at a discount."[132]

Strouss' was known for its elegant packaging, samples of which are featured in this photograph. *Courtesy of Mahoning Valley Historical Society.*

Commissions alone, however, do not fully explain the level of courtesy and personal attention that customers received. Sally Absalom, who later worked for the Strouss' Division, described the kindness she received when visiting the store as a teenager. "Everybody was always friendly," she recalled. "They were always knowledgeable about the merchandise, and it made you feel like they liked you coming in to see them." Mrs. Absalom was especially impressed with veteran salesperson Marge Riles, who staffed a kiosk on the main floor that featured items bound to appeal to younger shoppers. "They'd go to great pains to show you something that really wasn't very expensive," she said. "They were always willing to help you, regardless of how much you wanted to spend."[133]

Upon purchasing an item, customers came to expect that it would be attractively packaged. As a child, insurance worker Janet DeCapua recalled that "purchases were carefully boxed with tissue paper and wrapping, and most packages were delivered to customers' homes through a delivery service."[134]

In the wake of the merger, the Strouss-Hirshberg Co. also maintained a family-like corporate culture that encouraged employees to treat their jobs as careers. The firm continued its policy of supporting what it called "Ten- and Twenty-

In 1950, employees participated in a skit to celebrate Strouss-Hirshberg's seventy-fifth anniversary. This scene re-creates the moment that Isaac Strouss and Bernard Hirshberg established their fruitful partnership. *Courtesy of Mahoning Valley Historical Society.*

Five-Year Clubs," which were reserved for employees who demonstrated a long-term commitment to the company. Every year, dinners were held to welcome new members into these organizations, while at the same time honoring those who had served with distinction over the years.

On January 4, 1951, when the clubs assembled for their annual dinner at the ballroom of Youngstown's Ohio Hotel, 61 participants had worked for the company for a quarter of a century or longer, and only 11 of these were retired. Meanwhile, 129 of those who participated had worked for the firm for at least a decade. Given that this particular gathering coincided with the company's seventy-fifth anniversary, the firm's vice-president, George V. Thompson, offered a special introduction. "It is a privilege for me and an honor indeed to have a part in the observance of this important milestone," Thompson wrote in an introduction to the program. "On behalf of all those who hold positions of leadership in our Youngstown store, as well as our stores in New Castle, Warren and Salem, I offer heartiest congratulations and express the hope that we may all continue to serve with that high degree of loyalty and sincerity of purpose that has played such an important part in the growth of our splendid store."[135]

In the course of the evening, Thompson himself announced his imminent retirement from the company after forty-four years of service. Following a

Dancers dressed as elevator operators perform a musical number to mark the store's seventy-fifth anniversary. *Courtesy of Mahoning Valley Historical Society.*

presentation of watches and pins to employees who had been inducted into the clubs, Thompson himself received a loving cup from Jerold Meyer, the store's general manager and general merchandising manager.[136]

Thompson's departure from the Strouss-Hirshberg Co. coincided with a lavish celebration of the firm's seventy-fifth anniversary, an event that featured dramatic reenactments of episodes in the company's history, humorous sketches and choreographed musical numbers, one of which included dancers who were dressed as elevator operators. The evidence suggests that the company's sense of identity had survived the merger fully intact.

Central to this unique culture was a preference for hiring from within, which provided ambitious employees with chances for advancement. Personnel Director Glen Anderson, whose story exemplifies the long-standing influence of this culture, retired in December 1958 after nearly thirty-nine years. Like many of those who eventually rose to executive positions, Anderson had started as a part-time clerk in about 1917. When George Thompson invited him to work as an assistant to Louise Franz, then the company's training director, Anderson distinguished himself and "rose rapidly," assuming the position of director within eight years. He was among many older employees who recalled when the firm was small enough to greet every employee by

The Strouss' Division took conscious steps to create a familial atmosphere for its employees. In 1956, these employees turned out to play bingo at an event held at the Idora Park ballroom. *Courtesy of Mahoning Valley Historical Society.*

name. "You'd see them every day," he stated to a *Vindicator* reporter, "but now with 1,850 you might see an individual only twice a month."[137]

Interestingly, when Sally Absalom joined the staff of the downtown department store more than two decades later, she found its esprit de corps largely intact. "Oh, people were proud…to be associated with Strouss'," Mrs. Absalom recalled. "They would say, 'Oh, I worked at Strouss'—and that was important." She added, "They were good enough to be employed at what was considered the best store in town."[138]

Yet, the Strouss-Hirshberg Co. was eventually forced to respond to external developments that were affecting the community as a whole. As the 1940s drew to a close, there was a dramatic shift in population from the city to the suburbs, brought on partly by the flight of the middle class to affordable and "safe" housing but also by the return of veterans who wanted to start families. The dramatic growth that Youngstown had experienced in the first two decades of the twentieth century would not be replicated in the decade that followed World War II. By 1950, for instance, Youngstown's population was recorded at 168,000, which reflected an extremely modest increase from the 1940s census record of 167,200.[139]

Signage for Strouss' Men's Store competes with other neon signs along bustling Phelps Street in 1957. *Courtesy of Mahoning Valley Historical Society.*

This trend would continue, despite the postwar "baby boom," and by 1954, a *Vindicator* estimate revealed that the city's population had risen modestly to 168,330, a gain of merely 610 residents over a ten-year period. Meanwhile, the survey indicated that the neighboring suburbs of Austintown and Boardman saw their respective populations virtually double during the same period.[140]

Significantly, local businessman and entrepreneur Edward J. DeBartolo recognized this trend as an opportunity and began to build subsidized homes for returning veterans in Boardman Township, just south of Youngstown. DeBartolo correctly predicted that "the new occupants might prefer shopping at accessible California-style arcades to making the long drive to downtown Youngstown." While critics predicted that the developer's enterprise would fail, referring to it as "DeBartolo's 14 stations of the cross," they were quickly proven wrong.[141] Overall, the trends that subtly unfolded in the 1950s would become more pronounced in the decades to come, and they would change the face of downtown Youngstown, along with the local retail sector as a whole.

CHAPTER 4

Soaring into the Sixties and Seventies

The early 1960s constituted a period of optimism not witnessed since the decade of the 1920s, and notably, both eras featured large youth populations that insisted upon novelty and change. The spirit of the '60s was reflected, to some extent, in the presidential race of 1960. Richard M. Nixon, the Republican candidate, assured the country, "You never had it so good," while the Democratic candidate, John F. Kennedy, asked the citizenry to join him in "building a better America."

In Kennedy's stump speech in Youngstown, Ohio, on October 9, 1960, he framed the upcoming election as a stark choice of opposites. "The division is clear," Kennedy stated, as he stood on the balcony of the Tod House near Youngstown's Central Square. "It is between those who stand still and those who move forward, between those who look to the past, between those who want to protect a special position or special interest, and those who work for the people." He appealed to the crowd for their vote by referring to President Abraham Lincoln's winning of Ohio: "In 1864 Abraham Lincoln, when awaiting the returns of the election of 1864, finally heard that Ohio had voted for him, he sent out a word, 'Thank God Ohio has saved the Union.'"[142]

While Kennedy lost the battle for Ohio, he narrowly won the war for the presidency—a signal, perhaps, that the nation was ready for change. During his tragically truncated term, Kennedy managed to cut taxes and increase government spending, accelerating an economy that had stagnated during the years of 1957 to 1961. In the wake of these encouraging developments, the Strouss-Hirshberg Co. continued to

This undated photograph, probably taken in the 1960s, shows the remodeled West Federal Street entrance. To modernize the store's appearance, architects removed the arched entrances, along with the arcade of display windows. *Courtesy of Mahoning Valley Historical Society*.

expand its retail business, and by 1963, it would even establish a presence in Edward J. DeBartolo's Boardman Plaza.

The area, at large, was apparently swept up in a mood of idealism, and there was much talk of building a brighter future. In June 1960, about four months before Kennedy's speech on the square, the Youngstown Jewish Federation celebrated its twenty-fifth anniversary, announcing, among other things, that a home for senior citizens would soon rise near the sprawling complex of the Jewish Community Center. (The center itself had been dedicated to the memory of Clarence J. Strouss Sr., seven years after his death.)[143]

Two years earlier, in March 1958, crowds had gathered outside newly rebuilt St. Columba's Cathedral to watch "the spectacle of a helicopter raising a 300-pound aluminum cross atop the bell tower."[144] The new structure towered over the city's retail district like a bold (if controversial) monument to postwar modernity, and the downtown itself remained the bustling center of the city. "I remember driving to my father's store, which was on the lower east side," said Richard Scarsella. "We would go through East and West Federal Streets, and you would see all the buses that were

An early morning shot of Strouss-Hirshberg's West Federal Street entrance shows one of many buses that stopped at the store each day to drop off shoppers from around the community. *Courtesy of Mahoning Valley Historical Society.*

Many former customers remember the elegant mural located above the exit of the downtown Strouss' store. *Courtesy of Mahoning Valley Historical Society.*

lined up in front of Strouss' and McKelvey's, in particular." The district, he added, functioned as a local center of transportation. "I remember the old transit garage downtown," Scarsella said. "And, of course, you still had railroad depots that had trains coming through several times a day."[145]

Some of those trains were filled with shoppers who traveled from other parts of northeastern Ohio and western Pennsylvania. Terry O'Halloran, a local resident who spent a portion of his youth in nearby Sharon, Pennsylvania, recalled riding the train with his family and getting off within a block of Strouss' rear entrance on Commerce Street. He remembered the trip as an "adventure" that concluded with the "sights and sounds" of Strouss' Department Store.[146]

Although the exodus from the city was well underway, suburban dwellers continued to travel downtown on a regular basis. Among them was James Doran, who spent much of his youth in neighboring Boardman Township. "I can remember what a treat it was to walk down from the corner of our street, Brookfield and Glenwood Avenues, about nine houses, to get on a bus with my mom and my brothers," Doran said. "We'd go to different stores with my mom, primarily Strouss', and look for different things…and then, a real treat was to go to Raver's [Restaurant] for lunch." He noted that the trip often concluded with a film at one of the district's numerous movie palaces.[147]

As it turned out, however, the 1960s would unfold as a period of conflict and unrest, at home and abroad. Long-standing frustrations over racial inequality gave rise to the civil rights movement, and Americans would eventually be divided by polarizing issues, including the Vietnam War.

Nearly two years to the day of John F. Kennedy's stump speech in downtown Youngstown, the nation found itself embroiled in the Cuban missile crisis. James Doran vividly recalls the Christmas that came in the wake of that crisis. "I went down to the Erie Lackawanna [Terminal] with some good friends of my parents," he recalled. The group planned to meet Doran's grandparents, who were coming in from Minnesota for the holidays. "We had some time to kill, so my dad's friend…asked if I wanted to walk around in Strouss', and we did." As they perused the elaborate window displays and enjoyed the seasonal atmosphere, they solemnly discussed how close the world had come to disaster. "This was in December of 1962," Doran said. "And a lot of people wondered if there would be a Christmas."[148]

Meanwhile, unsettling changes were taking place in cities across the country, as more people retreated to the suburbs. "At some point, this has happened to every major American city, I think," Youngstown native Ben Lariccia said. "The signal was given…and upwardly mobile white people should not be living in downtown."[149] A trend toward suburbanization became more pronounced as the decade continued, and in 1965, the Ohio Department of Development reported that Youngstown's population had fallen from 166,689, in 1960, to 164,242, in 1964, reflecting a decline of 2,447.[150]

More sobering signs were evident in the community's stagnating industrial sector. While local steel companies like Youngstown Sheet & Tube moved their headquarters to outlying communities, actual steel production continued to take place in outmoded factories based in Youngstown and nearby Struthers and Campbell, Ohio. As scholar Thomas G. Feuchtmann observed, many of the mechanisms used in local steel production "could probably qualify as industrial antiques." He noted that a "1908 vintage steam engine with a 22-foot flywheel" continued to serve as the primary power source of one U.S. Steel facility until it closed in 1979.[151]

Lariccia personally encountered a trend toward industrial disinvestment when he worked for a local industrial firm as a young man. "As I got into my late teens and early twenties, I worked summers at Youngstown Foundry & Machine [Company] as a helper," he recalled. "And aside from the assembly

Trucks deliver air-conditioning equipment to one of Strouss-Hirshberg's receiving centers, which were located on West Wood Street and West Rayen Avenue, just north of the downtown area. *Courtesy of Mahoning Valley Historical Society.*

plant, the machine shop was ancient—just very, very, very old." While he acknowledged that he came across some modern equipment, his overall impression was "that no reinvestment was going on in the industrial area of Youngstown, no new plant buildings that I can remember."[152]

The implications of these trends, however, would not become plainly evident until the late 1970s. Throughout the '60s and early '70s, most observers regarded the city as reasonably vibrant, and the downtown continued to draw people from around the metropolitan area. The Strouss' Grille, a lunch counter on the corner of Commerce and Phelps Streets, always appeared to be crowded. "The Grille, of course, was a kind of social meeting spot," recalled Richard Scarsella. "You could walk in and you might be seated next to the mayor or Esther Hamilton, famed *Vindicator* gossip columnist."[153]

Overall, the Strouss-Hirshberg Department Store, now known almost exclusively as Strouss', offered a wide variety of amenities that set it apart

This 1960s photograph of Strouss' entrance offers a clear view of downtown Youngstown's Central Tower and McCrory's five-and-dime store. West Federal Street would eventually be closed off to make way for the Federal Plaza. *Courtesy of Mahoning Valley Historical Society.*

from most suburban retail outlets. At the peak of its development, the flagship store featured services including a framing shop, a beauty salon, a travel agency, a wig salon, a bridal registry, a photographic studio, a post office and a tire center.

The downtown store and its branches even sponsored periodic fashion shows, which had been a fixture of the Strouss-Hirshberg Co. as far back as the early twentieth century. "That was all part of the customer service at the time," recalled Mary Ann Senediak, who worked as a buyer at the store. "So, if you were to come shopping, you had your meal, you could plan your vacation, you could buy your Christmas gifts, you could arrange to have them delivered free of charge (through Anderson Delivery, at that time) and you could stop by at the bakery or stop and eat while your shoes were being repaired on the lower level."[154]

Moreover, the store's outstanding customer service involved steps that would be unheard of today. Sally Joseph, who worked in the fifth-floor glassware department in the late 1960s, indicated that customers occasionally took advantage of the store's generous policies. "Sometimes people brought in items for return that they had already used, and there were some cases where customers hadn't even removed traces of wine from the bottom of crystal glasses," she said. "My department would take them back anyway, even though they couldn't resell them."[155]

Customers also benefited from periodic sales that featured quality merchandise. "In those days, a product would come in at a particular retail price," recalled Patricia Sveth, who worked in the young men's department, on the mezzanine. "And once we sold a particular quantity of it (and at that time I think it was a third), they had made their money on it, and then prices would be really slashed." Ms. Sveth noted that her department often held ten-cent jean sales, which enabled mothers shopping for their children to purchase ten pairs of "name-brand" jeans for a dollar. "If you were lucky enough to have an odd size, you could pick fabulous articles of clothing up for a couple of dollars," she added. "It wasn't something you thought was inferior or brought in just for the sale. The sale was on the regular merchandise that they had, and it was national brands."[156]

Meanwhile, the store maintained a family-like corporate culture that many former employees recall with affection. Jack Thorne, who worked in the mezzanine's camera department during the 1960s, has fond memories of salesperson Val Luca, who had an "encyclopedic knowledge" of cameras and was aware of the latest innovations. After guiding a customer through a sale, Luca would often gesture to Thorne and say, "Now, let this young gentleman ring you up," which ensured that Thorne would get credit for the sale. "He was a super guy," Thorne said.

Perhaps his closest friend on the staff was Stanley Strouss, who ran the Strouss' Music Center, located on Wick Avenue next to the Masonic Temple. After work, Thorne occasionally met Strouss at a coffee shop located south of the Masonic Temple. The two men shared a love of polo, and Thorne often participated in polo matches held at Strouss's home on Warner Road, in Liberty Township. They were frequently joined by Stanley's brother, Albert "Burt" Strouss, an aspiring veterinarian, and salesperson Emerson "Emmy" Williams, who served as an announcer during polo matches. "The Mahoning Valley Polo Association would never have continued without Stanley Strouss," Thorne said.[157]

Many former employees, including Thorne, fondly recall Eleanor Scannell, who served as personnel director and, later, as employee liaison. "She was straight out of the movies," said Ray Laret, who worked in the central receiving department, beneath the store's parking garage. "I mean, you could run across her, and she'd call you by your first name. As a matter of fact, I think she always played Mrs. Claus in the Thanksgiving Day parade—very bubbly, very jubilant."[158]

Sally Absalom, who began as a part-time worker and rose to become manager of employee benefits, noted that even the store's executives were friendly, particularly Fred Gronvall, who came aboard as vice-president and general merchandise manager in 1967. "He would know if Pearl, who did the gift wrapping, had a sick aunt," Mrs. Absalom recalled. "And if he was going through the store, which he did periodically, he'd stop and say, 'Pearl, how's Aunt Ann?'" Mrs. Absalom added: "He was personable. He knew everybody in the store…and he cared about them."[159]

At the same time, Strouss' continued to sponsor its annual "Ten- and Twenty-Five-Year Clubs" dinners at the ballroom of what was now referred to as the Pick-Ohio Hotel, with organizers developing each event around a particular theme. In 1962, for instance, General Manager Jerold Meyer welcomed new members to a banquet thematically tied to the Roaring Twenties. More than three hundred guests arrived at a ballroom that took on "the appearance of a speakeasy during [the] free and easy '20s, thanks to the club's decorating and arranging committees," the *Vindicator* reported.[160] The event's menu included a "Charleston Cocktail," "Ragtime Radishes," "Boop Boop De Du Vitamins" and a "Half-Baked Potato."[161]

The following year, in 1963, the clubs held a luau, which "featured such fare as poi, lomi-lomi, a suckling pig, roast loin of pork (with sweet and sour sauce), baked bananas and fresh speared pineapple centerpieces." Entertainment was

Although he worked chiefly as a men's clothing salesman, Joseph A. Mendozzi's striking appearance earned him a sideline as a model for Strouss' newspaper advertisements. This proof dates to the 1960s. *Courtesy of Benjamin J. Lariccia.*

provided by local politician and humorist Bob Hagan, "who regaled members with anecdotes of their fellow employees."[162] All participants at the event received Vanda orchid leis and corsages that were "flown by jet airliner direct from Hawaii."[163] In 1966, the event's organizers went with a more subdued "winter

An undated photograph of Strouss' appliance store, located on Youngstown's south side. This specialized retail outlet was opened shortly after the close of World War II. *Courtesy of Mahoning Valley Historical Society*.

wonderland" theme, and the keynote speaker was Bishop James W. Malone, who discussed the implications of the Second Vatican Council.[164]

These high-profile events were supplemented by daily amenities that included a full-scale employee cafeteria, located on the mezzanine, and a break room featuring leather Barcaloungers and subdued lighting. "You could go to a lounge and be completely disconnected from the atmosphere of your job and relax for a half hour," recalled Ray Laret. "They always provided newspapers and everything—reading literature."[165] Jack Thorne recalled that the department store retained a full-time nurse, Helen McCarthy, who "treated her job very seriously" and even wore a nurse's cap and cape to work.[166]

Yet, even as Strouss' continued to raise its standards, engaging in expensive remodeling projects and improving the level of its customer service, the surrounding downtown retail district was falling into disrepair. Many of the store's traditional competitors were in the process of closing their doors, and a number of cherished landmarks had fallen to the wrecking ball. By 1964, the Palace Theatre, an elegant structure located to the northeast of the Central Square, had shown its last film. The public was outraged when it learned of the city's plans to raze the building. "They knocked the Palace down because they had a better plan for that spot," recalled Ben Lariccia. "I remember reading the zoning notes: The Palace would be knocked down, and something else would be put in its place—and nothing was put in its place."[167] Patricia Sveth indicated she also remembered the event, adding, "It was a real shame, because that's where I saw *Hard Day's Night*."[168]

For observers like Lariccia, the removal of the old movie theater was a chilling sign of things to come. "When the old Palace went down, that was a psychological indicator, and nothing was renewed, and nothing was put in its place," he said. "That was a signal that said, 'Okay, people are leaving… and there's nothing here that's worth resuscitating.'"[169]

The disappearance of the Palace Theatre was followed by the loss of another downtown icon. In February 1970, Milton Simon, host and owner of the Mural Room, widely viewed as the district's most elegant restaurant, announced that the business would be closing. While the end may have been hastened by the *Vindicator*'s planned construction of an annex, which would eliminate much of the restaurant's parking space, Simon acknowledged "that for two years, night-time dining in downtown Youngstown has become a thing of the past, except for a few special occasions."[170]

While these developments reflected the movement of people out of the city and into the suburbs, they were brought on by an explosion of suburban retail outlets, restaurants and cinemas. Obviously, Strouss' officers and directors could not afford to ignore these trends. In 1970, when Edward J. DeBartolo opened the Southern Park Mall in Boardman, Ohio, Strouss' was among the new complex's "anchor" stores. One year earlier, in 1969, when William M. Cafaro opened the Eastwood Mall in neighboring Niles, Ohio, Strouss' also secured a visible presence at the site. Indeed, the firm had been quick to recognize the opportunities present in suburban communities, given that it had established a store at the Liberty Plaza (Liberty, Ohio) as early as 1948 and opened an elegant outlet at the Austintown Plaza (Austintown, Ohio) in 1967.

At the same time, Strouss' refrained from following the lead of other retail firms, which were rapidly abandoning urban areas and closing most of their "stand-alone" facilities. In 1969, one year before the closing of Youngstown's Mural Room, Strouss' announced plans to build a $150,000 restaurant on the fourth floor of the adjacent Wick Building. The plan was outlined by Fred Gronvall, president and general manager of Strouss', and Earl Brauninger, president of the Union Bank, which occupied the building. They revealed that the colonial-themed restaurant would be called the Western Reserve Room.[171] For many area residents, the restaurant would eventually fill the vacuum that had been created by the closing of the Mural Room.

This undated photograph offers a view of Strouss' parking garage and pedestrian walkway as they appeared in the 1970s. *Courtesy of Mahoning Valley Historical Society.*

Over the next few years, Strouss' leadership would demonstrate a commitment to the revitalization of the city's downtown area. On October 31, 1973, when the municipal government held a groundbreaking ceremony for the so-called Federal Street Mall, the master of ceremonies for the event was none other than Strouss' Fred Gronvall. The $1.7 million project, which paralleled similar efforts across the country, was designed to create a "pedestrian mall" that would enhance "shopper enjoyment and convenience." According to the plan, Federal Street, which ran east and west, would be closed to vehicular traffic, with Walnut and Phelps Streets, running north and south, serving respectively as the western and eastern borders. (Walnut Street and Phelps Streets would be open to emergency and service vehicles only.)

Meanwhile, Market Street, a north- and south-running thoroughfare that bisected the Federal Mall and ran through the Central Square, would remain open to vehicular traffic; however, crossing points for pedestrians would be located at quarter points on the square with traffic signals coordinated to ensure safety. The goal of what came to be known as "Federal Plaza" was to create "an overall feeling…of informality and casual flowing space, emphasized by brick walkways and pavements." According to the program for the groundbreaking ceremony, "A gateway effect with a water sculpture serving as the focal point will be created at the west entry to the mall off Central Square."[172]

Slightly less than a year after the groundbreaking ceremony, on October 5, 1974, the Federal Street Mall opened to the public with festivities that included skydivers, a parade, an antique car show, horse-and-buggy rides and a local arts and crafts show.[173]

Interestingly, Strouss' had its own plans for revitalization. Around the time of the completion of the Federal Street Mall, the division began a $1 million two-phase remodeling program of its flagship store. As the *Vindicator* reported, "The large spending program is indicative of the faith Strouss' has in the future growth potential of downtown Youngstown." It appeared they were not alone. Most of the businesses in downtown Youngstown had their own programs for improvements, including the Peoples Bank, Dollar Savings and Trust Co., Central Tower and the Union National Bank.

Strouss' distinctive logo is replicated to form a sundial design on this gift package dating to the 1970s. *Courtesy of Mahoning Valley Historical Society.*

Apparently, many of the Youngstown merchants and bankers saw the improvement of the downtown area and their own facilities as necessary to continuing their success. As Strouss' Fred Gronvall said at the time, "The downtown facility is our largest volume store and has shown a steady sales growth for the past five years." He added, "The magnificent transformation which has taken place in the downtown area during the past several years has been a great help in building our great downtown business and the large volume here enables us to offer our best services and largest assortment."

The first phase of the Strouss' renovation, which affected the main and third floors, reached completion in December 1975. The main floor benefited from such improvements as new parquet aisles, carpeting and fitting rooms. The third floor gained a new department for sportswear, and a gift-wrapping and alterations pickup was conveniently located near the bridge to the parking garage. A second phase of remodeling, which was scheduled to begin in early 1976, would involve the second floor and budget store with similar improvements.[174]

Despite such expensive efforts to attract shoppers to the downtown area, however, the retail district's gradual decline continued. Moreover, the failure of

Struthers, Ohio native Mary Lou (Wagner) Uray got her start as a fashion illustrator at Strouss-Hirshberg Co. and went on to publish illustrations in *Vogue* magazine. Before her death in January 2012, she was ranked by peers as one of the country's top fashion illustrators. *Courtesy of Mahoning Valley Historical Society.*

projects like the Federal Plaza was replicated across the country, as municipal governments struggled to implement strategies to preserve beleaguered city centers. "I don't know why, but that didn't work," Ben Lariccia observed. "Same thing in Philadelphia—we did that too…two blocks in Philadelphia, and then the stores went under and we went back to vehicular traffic."[175]

Even the availability of convenient, low-cost parking did not appear to solve the problem. Strouss', after all, maintained a large parking garage, located just north of its rear entrance on Commerce Street, and by the 1970s, an enclosed pedestrian bridge enabled shoppers to enter the store without having to deal with traffic.

Drawing on his own family's experiences, Reverend Deacon John C. Harris speculated that the mall's closing off of major thoroughfares irritated residents who had developed routines for downtown shopping. He recalled that his father had been accustomed to parking in a lot on Wood Street, just north of the downtown retail district. "Then he would go, himself, get the car, drive down to Federal [Street] and pick us up at the curb in front of Strouss'—and Federal Plaza kind of eliminated that," he explained. Meanwhile, the plaza apparently contributed to unforeseen developments that further alienated potential shoppers. "I think that it also encouraged a lot of vagrancy," Reverend Harris added. "There were a lot of benches, those curved concrete benches. I can remember, in the later years, seeing the different vagrants laying there, or sitting there and drinking; and that added to the…perception that it's just not a good place to be."[176]

Some observers contend that the negative impact of the Federal Plaza has been exaggerated. Undoubtedly, the most powerful blow to downtown revitalization efforts came in the late 1970s, with the collapse of the Youngstown area's core steel industry. Challenges facing the community's industrial sector became apparent as early as the 1940s and '50s, when consultants urged local manufacturers to engage in "industrial diversification."[177] Despite such warnings, however, the community remained heavily invested in steel. Local civic and industrial leaders, in an effort to shore up the industry, even "sought federal funding to build a canal linking Lake Erie to the Ohio River Valley through Youngstown."[178]

The beginning of the end of Youngstown's steel industry, as it had existed up to that point, came in January 1969, when the New Orleans–based Lykes Corp. engaged in a hostile takeover of Youngstown Sheet & Tube, borrowing $150 million in bank loans and issuing about $191 million in debentures to finance the move.[179] As a result, the newly merged company "assumed a debt liability of nearly $350 million."[180]

This undated photograph of a display window captures the dramatically new fashions of the early 1970s. *Courtesy of Mahoning Valley Historical Society.*

Not surprisingly, Lykes Corp. failed to invest in upgrading Youngstown Sheet & Tube's facilities, plundered its resources and sent the steel company into a downward spiral from which it would never recover. On September 17, 1977, representatives of Lykes Corp. announced the closing of the firm's sprawling facility in neighboring Campbell, Ohio, along with plants in nearby Struthers. The Campbell shutdown alone resulted in the loss of five thousand jobs in the Youngstown area, and it would be the first in a series of crippling blows to the local economy.[181]

The shutdowns in Campbell and Struthers were followed by the staged withdrawal of U.S. Steel in 1979 and 1980, which culminated with the closing of its facilities in neighboring McDonald, Ohio.[182] More closings came with the bankruptcy of Republic Steel in the 1980s, ensuring that, within a few years, the "Steel Valley" (which comprised Mahoning and Trumbull Counties in Ohio and portions of western Pennsylvania) would lose about forty thousand manufacturing jobs.[183] Overall, the adverse impact of deindustrialization on the Strouss' Division of the May Co. would be difficult to exaggerate.

CHAPTER 5

Rainbow's End

On August 3, 1984, Fred L. Gronvall announced his retirement as chairman and chief executive of the Strouss' Division of the May Co. His retirement coincided with his sixtieth birthday, and the former executive indicated he had served with the division for seventeen years, which included fifteen years as chief executive. "I have been at this job longer than most people have been in this business," he said. "And that's a long time." The *Vindicator* reported that, in 1983, Gronvall's last full year with the Strouss' Division, its nine branches had witnessed "record sales of $103.6 million."

Apart from his success as a division leader, Gronvall had also succeeded in conforming to the standards of Strouss' unique corporate culture. Over the years, he had proven himself to be a personable and caring leader who was also capable of making difficult decisions. Newspaper articles suggest that Gronvall was as active within the community as he was within the division itself. A strong supporter of the local Boy Scouts, he also served as president of the Youngstown Board of Trade and Youngstown Area Chamber of Commerce. In addition, Gronvall was a trustee for several business and charitable organizations.[184]

Upon his arrival in the Youngstown area, Gronvall seemed determined to develop meaningful local connections. "I was the one that helped him to get to know people and to find a home when he first arrived here from Cincinnati," said former Strouss' executive C. Clark Hammit. "We became very close friends, and our wives were also very close," he added.[185]

Nine years earlier, Gronvall had met with Youngstown mayor Jack C. Hunter outside the downtown department store to accept a congratulatory resolution on the firm's centennial.[186] While he respected the Strouss' Division's rich past, however, Gronvall remained focused on the future. Within a year, the chief executive had announced plans to expand the division's store at the Liberty Plaza by 40 percent, while also pursuing an ambitious remodeling program that would achieve "an atmosphere of elegance and spaciousness."[187]

The project coincided with a major remodeling of the downtown store, along with the division's participation in a collective effort to revitalize the city's traditional retail district. Overall, Gronvall's seventeen years with the division had been

This late 1970s photograph shows Strouss' pedestrian walkway, which served as a bridge between the department store and a large parking garage on the north side of Commerce Street. *Courtesy of Reverend Deacon John C. Harris.*

extraordinarily eventful. Among other things, he witnessed the establishment of a 79,000-square-foot store at the Austintown Plaza, a 135,000-square-foot store at the Eastwood Mall, a 145,000-square-foot store at the Southern Park Mall and a 106,000-square-foot store at the Shenango Valley Mall in Sharon, Pennsylvania. Despite the adverse conditions created by the collapse of the region's steel industry, Gronvall could scarcely have predicted that the Strouss' Division would disappear within two years of his retirement.

Although the Strouss' Division had remained profitable, the May Co. was gradually shifting its focus from free-standing stores to mall-based retail outlets, and customers who continued to shop at the flagship store in

This collection of memorabilia—including a charge card, button and gift package—reflects Strouss' streamlined image in the late 1970s and early 1980s. *Courtesy of Mahoning Valley Historical Society.*

downtown Youngstown began to notice unsettling changes. "At one time, downtown Strouss' had the better merchandise, and the suburban locations in the plazas…did not have the better quality, the deeper selections, the size range," recalled Richard Scarsella. "As the years went by, into the '60s and '70s, it reversed; Boardman began to have the higher-end, deeper selections, the sizes and colors."[188]

Meanwhile, the Strouss' Division, as a whole, was struggling to keep pace with a changing youth market that had largely abandoned the formal styles of the past. Patricia Sveth recalled that, in the late 1970s, she was directed to set up one of the division's "Rivet" shops, which specialized in Levi's jeans. "When they transferred me from downtown out there, I was very excited, because it was a brand-new store," she noted. "We sold a lot of jeans and moved the merchandise."

Ms. Sveth added, however, that she left the area a few months later to accept a position in Florida, and by the time she returned, a year and a half later, the shops were no longer in business.[189] Mary Ann Senediak also recalled this unsuccessful bid for the youth market. "At that time…they had every style from the basic 501 (which is a five-pocket jean) to a fashion jean," she explained. "As your mass merchandisers, your discounters, came along with lower prices of jeans, it was harder for a smaller store like the 'Rivet' to compete."[190]

At the same time, the metropolitan market was rapidly shrinking. Between 1970 and 1980, the population of Mahoning County—which includes Youngstown and several large suburban townships—fell by 7.1 percent, dropping from 304,545 to 282,813. The losses in Youngstown itself were even more dramatic, with the population plummeting from 140,509 to 112,146—a drop of 20.4 percent.[191] Within a few years, the cumulative effects of depopulation and deindustrialization were reflected in Youngstown's diminished ranking among U.S. cities. In 1984, the *Vindicator* noted that Youngstown, which had been the country's 45th largest city in 1931, ranked 145th nationally. In addition, the former "boomtown," which had once been the third-largest city in Ohio, had slipped to the position of seventh largest.[192]

This negative trend would continue. A 1984 study conducted by the New York–based research firm Dun & Bradstreet Corporation ranked Youngstown as twenty-third among the country's twenty-five fastest-shrinking metropolitan areas in the period stretching from 1980 to 1983.[193] The study estimated that the Youngstown area experienced a 1.8 percent drop in population between 1980 and 1983.[194] Then, in 1985, the surrounding Mahoning County was ranked fourteenth in population loss in the country.[195]

To the alarm of civic leaders, researchers anticipated that the situation would worsen over time. A preliminary report issued by the Ohio Data User's Center, a research institute connected to Ohio's Department of Development, forecasted that depopulation would continue into the next century. The report projected that Mahoning County, which recorded 289,487 people in 1980, would have just 248,530 people in 1995 and only 229,687 by the year 2010.[196]

By the mid-1980s, Strouss' was the only major retail outlet operating in downtown Youngstown, and the absence of other attractions contributed to a further decline in customers. "When you would go into Strouss', it was very attractive," recalled Reverend Deacon John C. Harris. "But there wasn't much reason to leave the store and to go down the street any longer." The daylong excursions that he remembered from his youth were no longer possible. "Now, you would just go down, you would park in the garage, cross the pedestrian bridge into the store, do what you had to do and then get out of there," Reverend Harris said.

Mechanized figures like these continued to find a place in Strouss' holiday window displays during the 1980s. These animated puppies were featured in a display organized under the theme "It's a Good Life." *Courtesy of Reverend Deacon John C. Harris.*

Despite these changes, however, the Strouss' Division struggled to maintain cherished downtown traditions, including the annual Thanksgiving Day parade, which featured a last-minute appearance by Santa Claus. Many Youngstown-area residents who recalled the event from their own childhoods traveled to the downtown to share the experience with their children.

Reverend Harris, whose youngest son was born in 1983, attempted to turn the event into a family tradition. The parade, which was co-sponsored by local radio stations, drew the participation of marching bands and cheerleaders from local high schools, including South Range and Cardinal Mooney. "The kids would always be excited for that," Reverend Harris recalled. "They ran that right up, I think, until the store closed." In later years, he noted, he "didn't get the same feeling" when taking his children on holiday excursions to local malls and shopping plazas. Going downtown, he said, was "a continuity of what had been traditions in my own family," and his children, he added, "responded very well."

Perhaps the biggest attraction was the department store itself, with its "beautifully decorated" street-level floor. "They would do the swags of the lights all along the mezzanine rails," Reverend Harris recalled. "And there normally would be a big tree in the middle."[197] Yet, in family photographs

Raggedy Ann joins Santa Claus on an elegant float featured in Strouss' annual holiday parade during the early 1980s. *Courtesy of Reverend Deacon John C. Harris.*

that capture one of Strouss' last Thanksgiving Day parades, it is difficult to miss signs of the district's decay, including disheveled storefronts and vacant buildings.

Evidence of a significant change in the Strouss' Division's status emerged within two months of Fred Gronvall's retirement. Amid rumors of the downtown store's imminent closure, Larry Mickley, who succeeded Gronvall as president and chief executive officer, stated to a *Vindicator* reporter that "[the] Strouss department store in downtown Youngstown is alive and well and there are no plans to close its doors." Mickley was responding to comments made by the division's new chairman, John Rahilly, about the store's future that seemed to indicate it would close soon. "We're not closing the downtown store," Mickley claimed. "We are looking at the possibility of taking and relocating some merchandizing areas to make the store more attractive and exciting."[198]

While this statement may have reassured some observers, others were more inclined to interpret it as evidence of a future closing or, at the very least, a consolidation of floor space used for sales. This latter interpretation was largely supported by a January 29 *Vindicator* article in which Mickley unveiled remodeling plans for the downtown store. He indicated that a "major move" was scheduled for the sixth-floor housewares department,

Santa and Mrs. Claus wave to onlookers in downtown Youngstown during Strouss' annual Thanksgiving Day parade, which was held every November until the store's demise in 1986. Strouss' employee Eleanor Scannell traditionally portrayed Mrs. Claus. *Courtesy of Reverend Deacon John C. Harris.*

which would be relocated "to the fifth floor…to be integrated with china, silver, glass, gifts, and linens."[199]

In the same article, Mickley announced a $750,000 remodeling project for the store at the Southern Park Mall. His comments reflected an obvious shift of store investment, away from the downtown and toward the suburbs. Further evidence of the May Co.'s "disinvestment" in the downtown had surfaced earlier that month, on January 22, when Mickley and Rahilly confirmed rumors that the Western Reserve Room, the store's most elegant eating establishment, would close its doors in early February.

According to the *Vindicator*, Mickley claimed that the division's lease with Burdman Bros., the company that owned the Wick Building, "was 'no longer feasible' for either party." Mickley went on to say that the division's leadership intended "to look at the total downtown restaurant facilities and see what we can do to incorporate the Western Reserve influence into the existing facilities." When asked about the reasons for the restaurant's closing, Mickley stated, "It was not our space to do with as we pleased."[200]

In January 1986, the future of Strouss' became evident, as officials of the May Co. revealed their plans to merge the division with the Pittsburgh-

Cheerleaders from Youngstown's Cardinal Mooney High School participate in an annual holiday parade sponsored by Strouss' Department Store during the early 1980s. *Courtesy of Reverend Deacon John C. Harris.*

based Kaufman's Division. Jim Abrams, vice-president of corporate communications for the May Co., indicated that the merger would involve "no major changes from the customer's point of view." He added that any changes would "primarily involve a transfer of certain responsibilities handled in Youngstown to Kaufman's headquarters in Pittsburgh."

These responsibilities included "the buying of merchandise for the store, the advertising for the store, and eventually the distribution of merchandise." Abrams went on to explain that, in contrast to the current arrangement in which separate buyers purchased merchandise for the eleven Kaufman's stores and seven Strouss' stores, Kaufman's buyers would now "select merchandise for all 18 stores," a move that would give buyers of the merged division "increased buying power," while facilitating "a wider selection of better merchandise."

Meanwhile, William T. Tobin, president and chief executive officer of Kaufman's, addressed the concerns of those who questioned an arrangement in which Pittsburgh-based buyers would purchase merchandise for stores in Youngstown. "We can get rapid information, and we do exhaustive studies of the demographics of the areas we're in," Tobin asserted. "With the tremendous communications system we have, this should be no problem."[201]

At the same time, former employees of the Strouss' Division were learning more about their future. "Everybody was really upset…especially the salespeople," recalled former Strouss' executive Sally Absalom. "They could apply to other places for jobs, but if they didn't have an opening, you weren't going to get hired." The difficult position of many workers was compounded by the fact that they were approaching the end of their working life. "A lot of those women were like sixty years old and had worked there from the time they were twenty," Mrs. Absalom said.[202]

Mary Ann Senediak, who also worked as an executive at the downtown store, vividly described how she learned about the merger on January 2, 1986. "We had a large management meeting," she said. "The executives were told that the majority would receive severance packages, and some of the executives would be retained." She noted that Strouss' executives were also informed that their severance packages would not kick in until the end of January.

Not until January 31, 1986, did Ms. Senediak learn that her job had been "saved." In a subsequent meeting with Kaufman's executives, she was told that she had been assigned, with eight others, to close the flagship store in downtown Youngstown. "My job was to help coordinate all of the stock that we had," she explained. "We coordinated all the sales, and the sales started with taking an extra 25 [percent] off. Then, they moved to 33 [percent] off, then 50 [percent] off the ticket, then 75 [percent], then 90 [percent] off— and it was at that point they closed the store."

One of Ms. Senediak's final responsibilities was to remove items that had been left behind in the former executive offices—including staplers, scissors, binders and other equipment—and then to toss them into a large waste receptacle. As it turned out, she was the last person to leave the building, that is, besides operational workers. The experience, she recalled, was "devastating." "The Strouss' Department Store was such an iconic store in the downtown area," she said. "And when I started there, practically every [employee] had a family member that worked at Strouss' or one of the branches." She added, "And people, when you mentioned you worked at Strouss', they always told you, 'Oh, we loved those chocolate malts,' and that we were known for that, all over."[203]

Hope in the City

The closing of downtown Youngstown's Strouss' Department Store was a sad milestone in the community's history, and the local media recorded the event in grim detail. In June 1986, as the former flagship store (known fleetingly as Strouss-Kaufman's) wound down its final sale, a *Vindicator* reporter took note of the emotional gulf that separated grieving workers from shoppers who mechanically sorted through the discounted merchandise. The reporter noted that, as a "clerk on the third floor of the downtown Strouss-Kaufman's store tearfully hugged two workers farewell," perhaps for the last time, "preschoolers romped in the store's newly cleared floor space, unconcerned that a chapter in Youngstown's history was drawing to a close." Many shoppers, she added, were "as unconcerned as the children they brought with them as they rooted through what remained from the clearance sale."[204]

Yet, even at this stage, a plan was evolving to preserve the building, and civic leaders appeared determined to prevent the structure from going the way of long-vanished landmarks like the Palace Theatre. On the very day of the closing sale, Youngstown mayor Patrick J. Ungaro indicated he was expecting proposals for the building's reuse within a week.[205] One month later, in July 1986, Barry D. Kaufman, a regional vice-president for the May Co., expressed the firm's intention to "give" the building to the City of Youngstown. "We have looked really long and hard at this and still are prepared to move heaven and earth to make it a gift," Kaufman said. The May Co. official had already met with a six-member committee of civic leaders that had been organized by the mayor's assistant, Charles P. Saulino.[206]

Strouss' employees participated in annual outings at local recreational centers. This undated 1950s photo appears to have been taken at Idora Park on Youngstown's south side. *Courtesy of Mahoning Valley Historical Society.*

By January 1987, a plan had taken shape—the newly organized Strouss Building Association secured a lease on the structure while forming a partnership with the architectural firm of Buchanan, Ricciuti & Associates, which began the process of restoring the historic building's exterior. "It is an incredible building," said architect Paul J. Ricciuti, who indicated bids would soon be issued "for restoration of the exterior windows and masonry cleaning." Among the tenants already committed to leasing space in the building was Youngstown-based Phar-Mor, a chain of discount stores that planned to "move its headquarters on to the third floor," while also using part of the second floor.[207]

Over the years, the project to preserve the building would face its share of challenges. In 1992, for instance, Phar-Mor dissolved in a wave of scandal, depriving the facility of its largest tenant at that time.[208] Yet, the building prevailed, and it currently houses government offices, law firms and various retail outlets.

Local residents like Reverend Deacon John C. Harris are glad it's still there. "If you just stop and you look at the building, and look at the details…it's fascinating," Reverend Harris said. "I don't even know what architectural style the building is. I think that there are elements of the Italian Renaissance. There are Beaux Arts [influences]. There might even be a little bit of Art Deco there."

For Reverend Harris, however, the building's details call to mind those of a Gothic cathedral, and he takes delight in introducing the landmark to members of the rising generation. "When I've been downtown, and I've taken my grandson and some younger folks with me, I've talked to them about some of the architecture," he recalled. "And they look up at some of these buildings and go, 'Wow, that's amazing.'" Reverend Harris stressed the importance of helping young people to develop a "sense of history and culture," adding that they are unlikely to gain this sensibility during shopping expeditions at "a big box sitting along an interstate."[209]

At this point, the former Strouss-Hirshberg building isn't the downtown's only attraction. Visitors to the area have discerned a new vitality along West Federal Street, once the city's bustling retail district. The Federal Building, which stands one block west of the former department store, currently hosts a sleek restaurant-lounge, one of several new businesses that line the thoroughfare. Neighbors include a delicatessen, an Irish pub, a modern government building and the glistening DeYor Centre, an entertainment complex that occupies the site of the former Warner Bros. Theatre, whose restored façade looks much as it did in 1931 when it opened to the public. On the opposite side of West Federal Street stands the former confectionary of Harry Burt, who introduced the famed Good Humor Bar in the early 1920s. The refurbished three-story building will soon be reopened as the Mahoning Valley History Center.

Two blocks to the east stands the Youngstown Business Incubator (YBI), a nonprofit organization whose stated mission is "to accelerate the formation, cultivation, and success of technology-based business innovators."[210] A star member of the organization's portfolio is Turning Technologies, a company that develops leading assessment delivery and data collection solutions for learning environments. In 2007, the firm was ranked by *Inc.* magazine as the fastest-growing privately held software company in the United States and the eighteenth-fastest-growing privately held company overall.[211]

Indeed, the rapid growth of Turning Technologies was a factor in *Entrepreneur* magazine's decision, in July 2009, to cite Youngstown as one of the top ten cities in which to start a business.[212] YBI also oversees the National Additive Manufacturing Innovation Institute (NAMII), located a couple of blocks south on West Boardman Street. NAMII is part of the Obama administration's "We Can't Wait" initiative, and on August 16, 2012, the White House announced the launching of the "public-private institute for manufacturing innovation," which it framed as "part of its ongoing efforts to help revitalize American manufacturing and encourage companies to invest in the United States."[213]

Meanwhile, the downtown area has seen the rise of galleries, consignment shops, bookstores, upscale apartments and high-tech entertainment venues such as the Covelli Centre, which is located on the site of a former steel mill. The district is a far cry from the urban wasteland visitors encountered in the late 1980s and 1990s.

Patricia Sveth recalled that she was shocked when she learned about the response of visitors from the Soviet Union, who were part of a "sister city" exchange program during this period. "They took them downtown, and [the Soviet visitors] wanted to know when the war happened," she said. "So, downtown was, I guess, in pretty sad condition."[214] Reverend Deacon John Harris vividly described this period in the district's history. "I can remember how sad it was twenty years ago to walk down Federal Street," he said. "You'd have to cover your nose because of the stench from the buildings… the mildew, and the false fronts falling off of them."[215]

At this point, however, there are relatively few traces of blight, and many residents appear confident that the downtown is experiencing a comeback.

That said, older residents seem convinced that the new downtown will look very different than the vibrant district they recall from their youth. Although former resident Ben Lariccia said he missed the presence of retail outlets (and other businesses that offer products and services required for daily living), he was nevertheless encouraged by the fact that the district has reemerged as a public space where "people cross and meet and develop a connection."

He explained that his love for cities has been deepened by the words of his pastor at St. Gabriel's Episcopal Church in Philadelphia, who described the city as "an icon for the face of God"—that is, a symbol of human diversity. At the same time, he noted, she encouraged her congregation to "take seriously the fact that the Bible begins in a garden and ends in a city."[216] For Lariccia, the traditional urban center functioned as a space where people of various backgrounds came together and learned to coexist.

Such opportunities are relatively scarce today, said Josephine Houser, who described the contemporary shopping experience as "a mob scene." Like many of her generation, Mrs. Houser looks back fondly on a period when people seemed to show greater consideration to one another.

Significantly, many of those who reflect on their experiences at Strouss' Department Store find themselves drawn to small but memorable acts of kindness. Reverend Harris indicated he would never forget the thoughtfulness of Strouss' employee Ann Lotto, who introduced his daughter to her first sample of perfume. He recalled that whenever he and his wife, Sylvia, happened to meet the elderly woman, she never failed to recount their daughter's first visit to the cosmetic counter. "In spite of the work she had to do, she paid attention to a little girl," Reverend Harris said. "And I find that impressive."[217]

Notes

Introduction

1. "Thousands Help Launch New Strouss-Hirshberg's: Watch Airplane Drop Floral Tribute from Mayor, Then Inspect New Store," *Youngstown Vindicator*, November 2, 1926, 3.
2. "Strouss-Hirshberg to Erect $1,000,000 Home: Acquire 99-Year Lease on Most Valuable Real Estate in Heart of City—Ten or 12-Story Building Will Be Erected—Means Passing of Landmarks," *Youngstown Vindicator*, November 29, 1918, 1.
3. "Thousands Help Launch New Strouss-Hirshberg's: Watch Airplane Drop Floral Tribute from Mayor, Then Inspect New Store," *Youngstown Vindicator*, November 2, 1926, 3.
4. "New Strouss-Hirshberg's Opens: Crossroads Store Grows to Metropolitan Enterprise," *Youngstown Vindicator*, supplement, November 1, 1926.
5. Richard S. Scarsella, interview by the author, August 22, 2012, transcript, Ethnic Heritage Society Collection, #385, Mahoning Valley Historical Society, Youngstown, OH.
6. Josephine Houser, interview by the author, September 14, 2012, transcript, Ethnic Heritage Society Collection, #385, Mahoning Valley Historical Society, Youngstown, OH.
7. Ben Lariccia, interview by the author, August 22, 2012, transcript, Ethnic Heritage Society Collection, #385, Mahoning Valley Historical Society, Youngstown, OH.
8. Mary Ann Senediak, interview by the author, September 23, 2012, transcript, Ethnic Heritage Society Collection, #385, Mahoning Valley Historical Society, Youngstown, OH.
9. David Skolnick, "Downtown Rebound: Signs of New Life in Youngstown," *Youngstown Vindicator*, June 17, 2012, accessed September 23, 2012, http://www.vindy.com/news/2012/jun/17/downtown-rebound-signs-new-life-youngstown/.

10. David Skolnick, "Sealing the Deal on the Chevrolet Centre," *Youngstown Vindicator*, November 18, 2005, Sec A-1.

11. Don Shilling, "Dare to Dream? City's Potential Noted," *Youngstown Vindicator*, July 18, 2009, accessed April 27, 2011, www.vindy.com/news/2009/jul/18/dare-to-dream-city8217s-potential-noted/.

12. David Skolnick, "Realty Rises to Reality: If This Project Succeeds, It Would Lead to Other Upscale Housing Downtown, The Mayor Says," *Youngstown Vindicator*, August 20, 2009, accessed September 22, 2012, http://www.vindy.com/news/2009/aug/20/realty-rises-reality/.

13. Todd Franko, "Remaking Downtown Youngstown," *Youngstown Vindicator*, December 25, 2011, accessed September 22, 2012, http://www.vindy.com/news/2011/dec/25/keep-faith-in-the-city-keep-faith/.

14. Amelia Marinelli and Concetta Lariccia, interview by author, August 23, 2012, Poland, OH.

15. Patricia Sveth, interview by the author, August 28, 2012, transcript, Ethnic Heritage Society Collection, #385, Mahoning Valley Historical Society, Youngstown, OH.

16. Lariccia, interview.

CHAPTER 1

17. "Isaac Strouss Dies After Few Weeks' Illness: Week After Golden Jubilee Celebration Strouss-Hirshberg Vice-President Suffered Nervous Breakdown—Condition Became Critical After Cerebral Hemorrhage," *Women's Wear*, April 2, 1925.

18. "Honor Guard at Strouss Rites: Body of Merchant Will Lie in State Tomorrow," *Youngstown Telegram*, April 2, 1925.

19. "Eulogy Offered Isaac Strouss: Dr. Philo Says His Life Was Well Lived," *Youngstown Telegram*, April 4, 1925.

20. Esther Hamilton, "Strolling Around Town," *Youngstown Telegram*, April 3, 1925.

21. "Isaac Strouss Dies in Home: Noted Business Man Falls Victim to Stroke," *Youngstown Telegram*, April 1, 1925, 1.

22. "Story of Isaac Strouss, written by Clarence J. Strouss, April 1913," typewritten manuscript, Estate of Clarence J. Strouss Jr. Collection, #267, Mahoning Valley Historical Society, Youngstown, OH.

23. "Strain Proves Too Great for Aged Merchant: Death Follows Breakdown Which Came During Celebration of Company," *Youngstown Vindicator*, April 1, 1925.

24. Charles I. Cooper, "The Story of the Jews of Youngstown," *The Jewish Criterion*, October 29, 1918, 5.

25. "D. Theobald & Co.: One of the Oldest Firms in Youngstown," *Youngstown Vindicator*, supplement, April 29, 1893.

26. Irving E. Ozer, Harry Alter, Lois Davidow and Saul Friedman, *These Are the Names: The History of the Jews of Youngstown, Ohio, 1865 to 1990* (Youngstown, OH: Irving E. Ozer, 1994), 23.

27. "Story of Isaac Strouss."

28. Ozer et al., *These Are the Names*, 23.

29. "Rodef Sholom Marking Centennial: Ceremony Is Friday," *Youngstown Vindicator*, May 4, 1967.

30. Ozer et al., *These Are the Names*, 31.

31. Cooper, "The Story of the Jews of Youngstown," 5–6.

32. John Lycette, "So They Quit Their Jobs and Went into Business: It Was Start of Half Century Partnership of Messrs. Strouss and Hirshberg," *Youngstown Telegram*, March 7, 1925.

33. "Bernard Hirshberg Dies As Result of Accident Injuries: Vice President of Strouss-Hirshberg Co. Succumbs at Home; Struck by Automobile Two Years Ago," *Youngstown Telegram*, May 13, 1931, 1.

34. Cooper, "The Story of the Jews of Youngstown," 32–33.

35. "Bernard Hirshberg Pays Tender Tribute to Friend, Isaac Strouss," *Youngstown Vindicator*, April 2, 1925.

36. "Responses of the Founders Isaac Strouss and Bernard Strouss at the Golden Jubilee Banquet March 7th, 1925," program, Estate of Clarence J. Strouss Jr. Collection, #267, Mahoning Valley Historical Society, Youngstown, OH.

37. Ozer et al., *These Are the Names*, 17.

38. "David Theobald," *Youngstown Vindicator*, December 30, 1886, 5.

39. Lycette, "So They Quit Their Jobs and Went into Business."

40. "Strouss & Hirshberg: An Immense Youngstown Establishment Occupying an Entire Block—How It Has Succeeded," *Youngstown Vindicator*, supplement, April 29, 1893.

41. "Strain Proves Too Great for Aged Merchant: Death Follows Breakdown Which Came During Celebration of Company," *Youngstown Vindicator*, April 1, 1925.

42. "Bereavement of Mrs. Isaac Strouss," *Youngstown Vindicator*, April 29, 1893.

43. Solly Adams, "Meet C. J. Strouss: 'Three Presidents,'" *Youngstown Vindicator*, July 28, 1931.

44. "C.J. Strouss Dies, Funeral Monday: End Follows Collapse in Store Feb. 27," *Youngstown Vindicator*, March 8, 1947, 1.

45. "$10,000 Will Be Expended by Strouss & Hirshberg in Remodeling Their Store: Departments Will Be Enlarged and Changed, New Fixtures Purchased, Etc.," *Youngstown Vindicator*, January 20, 1902.

46. "Strouss & Hirshberg to Dissolve Partnership: Mr. B. Hirshberg Will Retire from Active Association in Firm," *Youngstown Vindicator*, June 28, 1906.

47. Lycette, "So They Quit Their Jobs and Went into Business."

48. "Anniversary: Fortieth Year for Strouss-Hirshberg Store Celebrated with Banquet," *Youngstown Vindicator*, March 20, 1915, 11.

49. "Strouss-Hirshberg to Erect $1,000,000 Home: Acquire 99-Year Lease on Most Valuable Real Estate in Heart of City—Ten or 12-Story Building Will Be Erected—Means Passing of Landmarks," *Youngstown Vindicator*, November 29, 1918, 1.

50. "Office of Local Concern in Yokohama Feared Destroyed," *Youngstown Vindicator*, 21, September 5, 1923.

51. Thomas G. Feuchtmann, *Steeple and Stacks: Religion and Steel Crisis in Youngstown* (Cambridge, MA: Cambridge University Press, 1989), 94.

52. "C.J. Strouss Makes a Happy Hit by Touching Up the Nation a Bit," *Youngstown Vindicator*, November 20, 1914, 3.

53. "Hospital Banquet Attracts Representative Assembly: Jollification Is as Successful as Formal Opening of Sunday Afternoon—Ohio Hotel Brilliant Scene When 350 Guests Foregathered for Sumptuous Dinner," *Youngstown Vindicator*, February 2, 1915, 3.

54. "Shock Absorber for His Favorite Mount Humane Contrivance by Local Horseman: Interest in Horseback Riding, Which Dwindled Because of Paved Streets, May Be Revived," *Youngstown Vindicator*, June 8, 1910.

55. "Strouss-Hirshberg Jubilee Opens as 600 Attend Banquet: Portraits of the Founders Presented, to Hang in New Store—Honor Guests and Dr. Philo Speak," *Youngstown Vindicator*, March 8, 1925, 1.

56. Celia McGee, "Tracking Down a Childhood Tale's Unhappy End," *New York Daily News*, September 15, 2004, accessed October 4, 2012, http://articles. nydailynews.com/2004-09-15/entertainment/18269545_1_lonely-doll-dare-portrait.

57. "Strouss-Hirshberg to Build Store: Work to Begin March 1, 1926," *Youngstown Telegram*, March 9, 1925, 1.

58. "Responses of the Founders Isaac Strouss and Bernard Strouss at the Golden Jubilee Banquet March 7th, 1925," program, Estate of Clarence J. Strouss Jr. Collection, #267, Mahoning Valley Historical Society, Youngstown, OH.

59. "Strouss-Hirshberg Jubilee Opens as 600 Attend Banquet: Portraits of the Founders Presented, to Hang in New Store—Honor Guests and Dr. Philo Speak," *Youngstown Vindicator*, March 8, 1925, 1.

60. "Rabbi Praises Isaac Strouss: Dr. Philo Eloquently Eulogizes Business Man Whose Funeral He Conducts," *Youngstown Vindicator*, April 5, 1925.

61. Cooper, "The Story of the Jews of Youngstown," 7.

62. "Eulogy Offered Isaac Strouss: Dr. Philo Says His Life Was Well Lived," *Youngstown Telegram*, April 4, 1925.

Chapter 2

63. John R. Rowland, "Youngstown's Purse: Growth of Population in Youngstown Pictured from U.S. Census Records," *Youngstown Telegram*, 9, March 7, 1930.

64. "Sees 470,000 Here in 25 Years: Ohio Bell Man Tells Club of City's Prospects," *Youngstown Telegram*, October 23, 1925, 7.

65. "FC131: Postwar Boom and Bust (1920–1929)," *The Flow of History: A Dynamic and Graphic Approach to Teaching History*, http://www.flowofhistory.com/units/etc/20/FC131, accessed October 8, 2012.

66. "Thousands Help Launch New Strouss-Hirshberg's: Watch Airplane Drop Floral Tribute from Mayor, Then Inspect New Store," *Youngstown Vindicator*, November 2, 1926, 3.

67. "New Strouss-Hirshberg's Opens: Crossroads Store Grows to Metropolitan Enterprise," *Youngstown Vindicator*, supplement, November 1, 1926.

68. "Birthdays—Golden Jubilee, Presented to Ann Moss on the Event of the Golden Jubilee of the Strouss-Hirshberg Co., March 9th, 1925, by Its

Founders," booklet, courtesy of Mary Lou Moss Godleski, Mineral Ridge, OH/ Milton, MA.

69. "Store Stuff," March 13, 1926, the Strouss-Hirshberg Co., newsletter, Estate of Clarence J. Strouss Jr. Collection, #267, Mahoning Valley Historical Society, Youngstown, OH.

70. "Isaac Strouss Memorial Fund," pamphlet, Estate of Clarence J. Strouss Jr. Collection, #267, Mahoning Valley Historical Society, Youngstown, OH.

71. "New Strouss-Hirshberg's Opens: Crossroads Store Grows to Metropolitan Enterprise," *Youngstown Vindicator*, supplement, November 1, 1926.

72. Ibid.

73. Ibid.

74. "Honor Strouss on Anniversary: Officers of Strouss-Hirshberg Give Surprise Party for President," *Youngstown Vindicator*, July 6, 1928.

75. "New Strouss Store Opens: S.-H. Co. Opens Third New Establishment, in New Castle," *Youngstown Vindicator*, September 14, 1929.

76. David F. Burg, *The Great Depression: An Eyewitness History* (New York: Facts On File), 8.

77. Ibid., 67–68.

78. T.H. Watkins, *The Hungry Years: A Narrative History of the Great Depression in America* (New York: Henry Holt and Company, 1999), 53.

79. Burg, *The Great Depression*, 86.

80. Benjamin Roth, *The Great Depression: A Diary* (New York: Public Affairs, 2009), 65.

81. "Bernard Hirshberg Dies As Result of Accident Injuries: Vice President of Strouss-Hirshberg Co. Succumbs at Home; Struck by Automobile Two Years Ago," *Youngstown Telegram*, May 13, 1931, 1.

82. Ibid.

83. Solly Adams, "Meet C.J. Strouss," *Youngstown Vindicator*, July 28, 1931.

84. "First Orthodox Group," *The Jewish Criterion*, October 29, 1918, 34.

85. "Temple Emanuel," *The Jewish Criterion*, October 29, 1918, 36–37.

86. "First of Race Settled Here in Early 1837: Families Migrate to West from Coast; Form Rodef Sholem in May, 1867," *Youngstown Vindicator*, March 27, 1938.

87. Ozer et al., *These Are the Names*, 93–94.

88. Ibid., 98–99.

89. "Strouss Known as Leader: Directs Youngstown Allied Jewish Campaign—Noted Speakers Coming," *Youngstown Vindicator*, October 26, 1930.

90. Ozer et al., *These Are the Names*, 131–32.

91. Ibid., 132–33.

92. Roth, *The Great Depression*, 86.

93. David E. Kyvig, *Daily Life in the United States, 1920–1940: How Americans Lived Through the Roaring Twenties and the Great Depression* (Chicago: Ivan R. Dee, 2001).

94. "Charcoaled Marshmallows and Cool Lake Provide Fun for Strouss Picnickers," *Youngstown Vindicator*, August 17, 1936.

95. C. Clark Hammit, interview by author, August 30, 2012, Youngstown, OH.

96. "The Strouss-Hirshberg Co., Youngstown, Ohio, Annual Report to the Shareholders, for the Period February 1, 1937, to January 31, 1938," brochure, Estate of Clarence J. Strouss Jr. Collection, #267, Mahoning Valley Historical Society, Youngstown, OH.

97. Howard M. Sachar, *A History of the Jews in America* (New York: Vintage Books, 1992), 450–55.

98. Eric L. Goldstein, *The Price of Whiteness: Jews, Race, and American Identity* (Princeton, NJ: Princeton University Press, 2006), 191.

99. Sachar, *A History of the Jews in America*, 522.

100. Letter to Clarence Strouss Sr. from Fred Kahn, July 1, 1939, Estate of Clarence J. Strouss Jr. Collection, #267, Mahoning Valley Historical Society, Youngstown, OH.

101. "The Strouss-Hirshberg Co., Youngstown, Ohio, Annual Report to the Shareholders, for the Period February 1, 1944, to January 31, 1945," brochure, Estate of Clarence J. Strouss Jr. Collection, #267, Mahoning Valley Historical Society, Youngstown, OH.

102. "The Strouss-Hirshberg Co., Youngstown, Ohio, Annual Report to the Shareholders, for the Period February 1, 1945, to January 31, 1946," brochure, Estate of Clarence J. Strouss Jr. Collection, #267, Mahoning Valley Historical Society, Youngstown, OH.

103. Ibid.

CHAPTER 3

104. Hammit, interview.

105. "Geo. V. Thompson to Retire from Strouss-Hirshberg Co.: Old Timers Honor Him After 44 Years There," *Youngstown Vindicator*, January 2, 1951, 2.

106. Hammit, interview.

107. Letter written by Clarence J. Strouss Sr. to his son, Clarence J. Strouss Jr., dated March 8, 1941, original, Estate of Clarence J. Strouss Jr. Collection, #267, Mahoning Valley Historical Society, Youngstown, OH.

108. "The Strouss-Hirshberg Co., Youngstown, Ohio, Annual Report to the Shareholders for the Year 1946 (February 1, 1946 to January 31, 1947)," brochure, Estate of Clarence J. Strouss Jr. Collection, #267, Mahoning Valley Historical Society, Youngstown, OH.

109. Houser, interview.

110. Amelia Marinelli, interview by author, August 23, 2012, Poland, OH.

111. James Gray Doran, interview by author, August 21, 2012, transcript, Ethnic Heritage Society Collection, #385, Mahoning Valley Historical Society, Youngstown, OH.

112. Senediak, interview.

113. Lariccia, interview.

114. Reverend Deacon John C. Harris, interview by author, August 18, 2012, transcript, Ethnic Heritage Society Collection, #385, Mahoning Valley Historical Society, Youngstown, OH.

115. Lariccia, interview.

116. Sally Absalom, interview by author, August 23, 2012, transcript, Ethnic Heritage Society Collection, #385, Mahoning Valley Historical Society, Youngstown, OH.

117. Scarsella, interview.

118. Lariccia, interview.

119. Harris, interview.
120. Scarsella, interview.
121. "Clarence Strouss Dies, Funeral Monday: End Follows Collapse in Store Feb. 27," *Youngstown Vindicator*, March 8, 1947, 1.
122. Ibid.
123. "Clarence J. Strouss," *Youngstown Jewish Times*, March 14, 1947, 4.
124. "Clarence J. Strouss: 'Faith of Our Fathers,'" eulogy presented June 2, 1947, at the meeting of Mahoning Saddle and Bridle Association by Paul B. Davies, typewritten manuscript, Estate of Clarence J. Strouss Jr. Collection, #267, Mahoning Valley Historical Society, Youngstown, OH.
125. "Strouss Stores Merging with May Co., Keep Name: Two-Thirds of Holders Give Consent," *Youngstown Vindicator*, March 5, 1948, 1.
126. "Notice of Special Meeting of the Strouss-Hirshberg Company Called to Be Held on Monday, March 29, 1948, 8:00 p.m.," original, Estate of Clarence J. Strouss Jr. Collection, #267, Mahoning Valley Historical Society, Youngstown, OH.
127. Letter to C.J. Strouss Jr. from the May Department Stores Co., July 3, 1948, original, Estate of Clarence J. Strouss Jr. Collection, #267, Mahoning Valley Historical Society, Youngstown, OH.
128. *Store Stuff*, weekly newsletter for the workers of the Strouss-Hirshberg Co., November 11, 1949, original, Estate of Clarence J. Strouss Jr. Collection, #267, Mahoning Valley Historical Society, Youngstown, OH.
129. "Esther Hamilton, Strouss Left Successful Family Business to Make His Own Mark in Insurance Field," *Youngstown Vindicator*, March 11, 1956.
130. Houser, interview.
131. Betty Swanson, interview by author, August 23, 2012, Boardman, OH.
132. Scarsella, interview.
133. Absalom, interview.
134. Janet Decapua, interview by author, September 14, 2012, Canfield, OH.
135. "The Strouss-Hirshberg Co. Twenty-Five Club and Ten Year Club Dinner," January 4, 1951, Ohio Hotel Ballroom, program, Estate of Clarence J. Strouss Jr. Collection, #267, Mahoning Valley Historical Society, Youngstown, OH.
136. "Geo. V. Thompson to Retire from Strouss-Hirshberg Co.: Old Timers Honor Him After 44 Years There," *Youngstown Vindicator*, January 2, 1951, 2.
137. Glenn Morris, "Glen Anderson, Personnel Director at Strouss-Hirshberg, Retires Jan. 1," *Youngstown Vindicator*, December 28, 1958.
138. Absalom, interview.
139. "Population Up 16,000 in County: Youngstown Is Expected to Hold Its Own in Census Report," *Youngstown Vindicator*, June 11, 1950, A-1.
140. "Shift to Suburbs Shown in Population Figures," *Youngstown Vindicator*, August 1, 1954, A-6.
141. Jonathan R. Laing, "King of Malls: Despite His Billions, Edward DeBartolo Remains a Shadowy Figure," *Barron's*, June 12, 1989, 8–30.

Chapter 4

142. "John F. Kennedy: Remarks of Senator John F. Kennedy, Youngstown, Ohio, Public Square, October 9, 1960," *The American Presidency Project*, http://www.presidency.ucsb.edu/ws/?pid=25745 (accessed October 15, 2012).

143. "Jewish Federation's 25th Anniversary," *Youngstown Vindicator*, rotogravure, June 5, 1960.

144. Anna Jean Schuler, "Opening of St. Columba Cathedral Signals Growth of Youngstown Diocese," *Youngstown Vindicator*, January 4, 1959, A-15.

145. Scarsella, interview.

146. Terry O'Halloran, interview, October 20, 2012, Boardman, OH.

147. Doran, interview.

148. Ibid.

149. Lariccia, interview.

150. "City Population Drops 2,447 in 4-Year Period," *Steel Valley News*, February 28, 1965, 1.

151. Thomas G. Feuchtmann, *Steeples and Stacks: Religion and Steel Crisis in Youngstown* (Cambridge, MA: Cambridge University Press, 1989), 18–19.

152. Lariccia, interview.

153. Scarsella, interview.

154. Senediak, interview.

155. Sally Joseph, interview by author, September 10, 2012, Boardman, OH.

156. Sveth, interview.

157. Jack Thorne, interview by author, September 2, 2012, Youngstown, OH.

158. Ray Laret, interview by author, July 28, 2012, transcript, Ethnic Heritage Society Collection, #385, Mahoning Valley Historical Society, Youngstown, OH.

159. Absalom, interview.

160. "Roaring '20s Is Theme for Strouss' Veterans: Hotel Is Scene of Party for 10, 25-Year Clubs," *Youngstown Vindicator*, February 1, 1962, 4.

161. "Strouss-Hirshberg's Annual 10 and 25 Year Clubs Roaring '20s Banquet, Wednesday, Jan. 31, 1962, Pick-Ohio Ballroom," program, Estate of Clarence J. Strouss Jr. Collection, #267, Mahoning Valley Historical Society, Youngstown, OH.

162. "Strouss' Has Luau for 10 and 25-Year Employees," *Youngstown Vindicator*, January 23, 1963, 14.

163. "'Aloha' Strouss-Hirshberg's Annual 10 and 25 Year Clubs Hawaiian Luai, Tuesday, January 22, 1963, Pick-Ohio Ballroom," program, Estate of Clarence J. Strouss Jr. Collection, #267, Mahoning Valley Historical Society, Youngstown, OH.

164. "Strouss' 10-25 Year Club, Tuesday, February 8, 1966, Hotel Pick-Ohio Ballroom," program, Estate of Clarence J. Strouss Jr. Collection, #267, Mahoning Valley Historical Society, Youngstown, OH.

165. Laret, interview.

166. Thorne, interview.

167. Lariccia, interview.

168. Sveth, interview.

169. Lariccia, interview.

170. Marie Aikenhead, "Mural Room to Close Doors," *Youngstown Vindicator*, February 22, 1970, A-20.

171. "Strouss Restaurant Planned in Wick Bldg.," *Youngstown Vindicator*, August 8, 1969.

172. "Federal Street Mall Groundbreaking, Oct. 31, 1973," program, Reuben McMillan Public Library, Youngstown, OH.

173. "Federal Plaza Opening Brings Out Thousands, *Youngstown Vindicator*, October 5, 1974, 1.

174. "New Look for Strouss Store: $1 Million Downtown Remodeling," *Youngstown Vindicator*, December 7, 1975.

175. Lariccia, interview.

176. Harris, interview.

177. Sean Safford, *Why the Garden Club Couldn't Save Youngstown: The Transformation of the Rust Belt* (Cambridge, MA: Harvard University Press, 2009), 70.

178. Ibid., 71.

179. Feuchtmann, *Steeples and Stacks*, 42–43.

180. Richard Bruno, *Steelworker Alley: How Class Works in Youngstown* (Ithaca, NY: Cornell University Press, 1999), 113.

181. Feuchtmann, *Steeples and Stacks*, 1–2.

182. Douglas R. Sease, "Closing of a Steel Mill Hits Workers in U.S. with Little Warning: Though They Keep Getting Incomes, Retaining Aid, Creation of New Jobs Lag," *Wall Street Journal*, September 23, 1980.

183. Bruno, *Steelworker Alley*, 149.

CHAPTER 5

184. Alyssa Lenhoff, "Retiring Strouss Officer Refuses to Take Credit for Many Deeds," *Youngstown Vindicator*, August 3, 1984.

185. Hammit, interview.

186. "City Honors Strouss on 100th Year," *Youngstown Vindicator*, May 9, 1975.

187. "Strouss Will Expand Liberty Plaza Store," *Youngstown Vindicator*, July 8, 1976.

188. Richard Scarsella, interview by author, September 22, 2012, transcript, Ethnic Heritage Society Collection, #385, Mahoning Valley Historical Society, Youngstown, OH.

189. Sveth, interview.

190. Senediak, interview.

191. "Mahoning Co.'s Census Shows 7.1 Percent Drop," *Youngstown Vindicator*, July 8, 1980, 6.

192. "Youngstown Is 145th Most Populous U.S. City," *Youngstown Vindicator*, May 1, 1984, 4.

193. "Youngstown and Steubenville Among Top 25 in Population Drop," *Youngstown Vindicator*, May 28, 1984.

194. Ibid.

195. "Mahoning Co. Ranks 14th in Population Loss in U.S.," *Youngstown Vindicator*, May 6, 1985.

196. Ernest Brown Jr., "Continued Area Population Drop Likely," *Youngstown Vindicator*, September 12, 1985.

197. Harris, interview.

198. Bertram de Souza, "Downtown Strouss Isn't Closed," *Youngstown Vindicator*, October 13, 1984.

199. David Wolf, "Strouss Unveils Downtown Renovations; Proposes Remodeling at Southern Park," *Youngstown Vindicator*, January 29, 1985.

200. Karen Guy, "Strouss Will Close Restaurant," *Youngstown Vindicator*, January 22, 1985, 2.

201. Patrick McCarthy, "May Co. Predicts Benefits from Merger," *Youngstown Vindicator*, January 3, 1986.

202. Absalom, interview.

203. Senediak, interview.

EPILOGUE

204. Mary Ellen Crowley, "Gone: Many Sad on Last Day for Store," *Youngstown Vindicator*, June 27, 1986, 1.

205. Bertram de Souza, "Youngstown Awaits Proposals on Site's Use," *Youngstown Vindicator*, June 27, 1986, 1.

206. Bertram de Souza, "Panel to Assess Plans to Utilize Strouss Building," *Youngstown Vindicator*, July 13, 1986.

207. William A. Alcorn, "Strouss Work Taking Shape: Plans for Historic Building, Bids for Tenants Advancing," *Youngstown Vindicator*, January 21, 1987.

208. M.A. Stapleton, "Filings Show Monus Is Worth 2.9 million," *Youngstown Vindicator*, November 24, 1992, 1.

209. Harris, interview.

210. Youngstown Business Incubator, website, http://www.ybi.org/ (accessed October 17, 2012).

211. William K. Alcorn, "Turning Technologies Rated Fastest Growing," *Youngstown Vindicator*, August 24, 2007, accessed October 17, 2012, http://www4.vindy.com/content/local_regional/314857892476897.php.

212. Don Shilling, "Dare to Dream? City's Potential Noted," *Youngstown Vindicator*, July 18, 2009, accessed October 17, 2009, http://www.vindy.com/news/2009/jul/18/dare-to-dream-city8217s-potential-noted/.

213. White House, "We Can't Wait: Obama Administration Announces New Public-Private Partnership Support," http://www.whitehouse.gov/the-press-office/2012/08/16/we-can-t-wait-obama-administration-announces-new-public-private-partners (accessed October 17, 2012).

214. Sveth, interview.

215. Harris, interview.

216. Lariccia, interview.

217. Harris, interview.

About the Authors

Thomas G. Welsh Jr. is an independent scholar and professional writer and editor based in Youngstown, Ohio. He is a member of the advisory board of "Steel Valley Voices," a web-based project to promote awareness of the community's diversity, and also serves on the Exhibit Advisory Board of the Mahoning Valley Historical Society. He is the author of *Closing Chapters: Urban Change, Religious Reform, and the Decline of Youngstown's Catholic Elementary Schools* (Lexington Books, 2011), which describes factors that led to the collapse of a parochial school system. Examples of his research have appeared in the *American Educational History Journal*. Before completing a doctorate in cultural foundations of education at Kent State University in 2009, he worked as a journalist in the United States, South Korea and Cambodia.

Michael K. Geltz is a professional writer and editor based in Youngstown, Ohio. His connection to the retail industry goes back to the early 1980s, when he worked in the retail construction industry in New York and New Jersey. In his youth, he worked as a pipefitter for U.S. Steel's Ohio Works plant and as a welder for General Motors, in Youngstown and Lordstown, respectively. In the 1990s, he served as a writer and web producer for many mid-cap companies as well as Fortune 500 giants like Disney Consumer Products in Burbank, California. He earned a graduate degree in English language and literature from Youngstown State University in 1994 and has contributed to technical manuals published by Microsoft Press. As the son of an English-born mother, he spent a portion of his formative years in Coventry, England, whose history as an industrial center has close parallels to that of Youngstown.

Visit us at
www.historypress.net